*The Complete*

# Passover Seder

*Table Companion*

the
**jewish**
LEARNING GROUP

# THE COMPLETE PASSOVER SEDER
# TABLE COMPANION

SECOND EDITION
Copyright ©2001-2006
The Jewish Learning Group, Inc.

Published by

Tel. 1-(888)-56-LEARN
www.JewishLearningGroup.com
Email: info@JewishLearningGroup.com

ISBN 1-891293-17-6

# Acknowledgements

To Rabbis Moshe Bogomilsky and Shlomo Lakin for providing many text resources for this project.

To Rabbi Sholom Ber Chaikin, for giving so selflessly of his valuable time to read, amend, and refine the material presented here.

To the countless people and lay-leaders who have read and re-read the manuscript and offered their creative ideas, advice, and whole-hearted encouragement.

A special thanks to everyone else who helped make this book possible, *thank you!*

We have devised the following transliteration system to help you accurately pronounce the Hebrew words of blessings and prayers:

| Hebrew: | Transliteration: | Example: |
|:---:|:---:|:---:|
| כ or ח | **ch** | **Ch**allah |
| ָ | **ö** | **O**f |
| ַ | **a** | Hurr**ah** |
| ֵּ | **ay** | Tod**ay** |
| ֶ | **e** | L**e**g |
| ְ | **'** | **A**vid |
| ׂ or וֹ | **o** | T**o**ne |
| ִ | **i** | K**ey** |
| ֻ or וּ | **u** | L**u**nar |
| ַי | **ai** | **Ai**sle |
| ָי | **öy** | T**oy** |

# *Table of Contents*

# A Passover Overview

The story of *Pesach* (Passover) is well known, how the Jewish people were slaves to Pharaoh in Egypt, how Moses led us out of bondage and received the Torah on Mount Sinai, and how, after forty years in the wilderness, we entered into the Promised Land.

## Liberation from *Mitzrayim* (Egypt)

For the Jews, "Egypt" represents more than just a place on the map. Egypt is a state of mind. The Hebrew name for Egypt is *Mitzrayim*, which is related to the word *Maytzorim* — meaning boundaries and limitations. For the Jewish people, to "escape from Egypt" means to overcome those natural limitations that impede the realization of our fullest potential.

The innermost essence of the soul is a spark of Godliness — infinite and unbounded. But the soul is in exile, in "Egypt" — restricted within this finite, material world. One person's Egypt may be most apparent in his selfish and base desires; another person may be enslaved to the constraints of his rational mind. Pesach is an opportunity to transcend our limitations and realize the infinite spiritual potential in every aspect of our lives.

# True Freedom

When God commanded Moses to bring the Jewish people out of Egypt, He proclaimed His ultimate purpose: "...that they shall serve God upon this mountain." Our liberation was not complete until we received the Torah on Mount Sinai. God's Torah and commandments are the keys to achieving true freedom — freedom not just from physical enslavement, but from all our limiting beliefs and behavior. The Torah shows us how to avoid the pitfalls that life presents us, and teaches us how to make this world a place of peace, harmony and happiness for all humankind.

# Matzah and Chometz

Pesach is known as the "Festival of Matzot." We are commanded to eat matzah on the first night of Pesach, and to rid ourselves of chometz — all bread and leavened food products — for the entire eight days of the holiday. This important commandment offers us great insight into the true nature of liberation.

The difference between leavened bread and matzah is obvious: whereas bread rises, the Pesach matzot are not permitted to rise at all. Our Rabbis explain that the "puffed up" nature of chometz symbolizes the character trait of arrogance and conceit. The flat, unleavened matzah represents utter humility.

Humility is the beginning of liberation, and the foundation of all spiritual growth. Only a person who can acknowledge his own shortcomings and submit to a higher wisdom can free himself from his own limitations. On Pesach, we are forbidden even the minutest amount of chometz, symbolizing that we should rid ourselves from the arrogance and self-centeredness within our hearts. By eating the Pesach *matzot*, we internalize the quality of humility and self-transcendence that is the essence of faith.

# Splitting the Sea

On the seventh day of Pesach, we commemorate the miracle of the splitting of the Reed Sea — the culmination of the Exodus from Egypt. With the Egyptian charioteers in hot pursuit, the Jewish people plunged into the sea; God "turned the sea into dry land," thereby creating walls of water on both sides, and allowed His people to pass through. Upon their crossing the sea, the water returned to its normal state, drowning the Egyptians.

Our Sages explain that the splitting of the sea symbolizes yet another phase in our spiritual journey toward true freedom. Just as the waters of the sea cover over and conceal all that is in them, so does our material world conceal the Godly life force that maintains its very existence. The transformation of the sea into dry land represents the revelation of the hidden truth that the world is not separate from God, but is in fact one with Him.

Often, after "leaving Egypt" — after we overcome our limitations and ascend to a higher level — we experience a rude awakening. We may have left Egypt, but Egypt is still within us: We still view life in terms of the values of a materialistic world. We must strive to become more fully aware of God's constant presence and influence in our lives, until "the sea splits" and our liberation is complete.

## "I Will Show You Wonders"

In the words of the Prophet Michah, God proclaims, "As in the days when you left Egypt, I will show you wonders." The Exodus from Egypt is the prototype for the final Redemption, when *Moshiach* (the Redeemer) will come, and slavery and suffering will be banished forever from the face of the earth.

Why, our Rabbis ask, does the verse say, "As in the days when you left Egypt," when in fact the Exodus took place on one day?

The answer is that true liberation is an ongoing process. The first steps out of "Egypt" are only the beginning. "In every generation," the Sages tell us, "and on each and every day, one is obligated to see himself as if he had gone out from Egypt that very day." All the lessons of Pesach must be applied daily: we must rid ourselves of arrogance and become humble; we must deepen our awareness of God, as though the Reed Sea has split; and we must strive to improve our conduct, as befits the nation that received the Torah on Mount Sinai. Every step we take toward Torah and mitzvot brings us closer to the revelations of the messianic age.

# The Final Redemption

The eighth day of Pesach is traditionally associated with our fervent hope for the coming of *Moshiach*, the messiah. The *Haftorah* (special reading from the Prophets) for that day contains Isaiah's famous prophecies about the messianic era: "The wolf will dwell with the lamb, the leopard will lie with the kid...they shall do no evil, nor will they destroy...for the earth shall be filled with the knowledge of God, as the waters cover the sea."

The Rambam (Maimonides) cites the belief in *Moshiach* as one of the thirteen essential principles of our faith. He explains in his codification of Jewish Law that Moshiach is a Torah Sage, who will lead the multitudes of Jewish people to the faithful observance of the Torah way of life. Eventually, he will rebuild the Holy Temple in Jerusalem, gather in the exiles to Israel, and usher in an age in which there is no hunger, war, jealousy or strife.

# Signs of Hope

In today's chaotic world, one may find the concept of imminent Redemption difficult to accept. We can take heart, however, from the story of Pesach. Back then, despite our abject subjugation at the hands of the world's most ruthless and powerful nation — a nation from which not even a single slave had ever escaped before — Redemption came swiftly, "in the blink of an eye," and we were free.

In recent times, we have witnessed remarkable events that even secular leaders have termed miraculous: The fall of communism, the Persian Gulf War, the exodus and ingathering of Jews to Israel from places of former oppression.

Today, the wealth of nations is indeed turning from creating weapons of destruction into means of construction and cooperation – the proverbial "sword into plowshares." Such developments – long prophesied as harbingers of a messianic age – strengthen our faith in *Moshiach's* imminent approach.

The last day of Pesach is a uniquely appropriate occasion for our heartfelt prayers for *Moshiach*: "...Even though he may tarry, still I anticipate his arrival every day." As Maimonides explains, it will be a time of peace and plenty for all humankind, a time when we will no longer have to struggle for a livelihood. "Delicacies will be as plentiful as the dust, and we will all be free to engage in spiritual pursuits – to deepen our knowledge of God, and to serve Him unhindered."

# *Preparing for Passover*

Pesach is a period of eight days for which we prepare many days, even weeks in advance. Why? For unique to Pesach is the Biblical commandment to eat matzah and the stringent prohibition against eating or possessing chometz.

## What is Chometz?

In the Torah's (Bible) narration of the exodus from Egypt we find the following passage:

> *"...Remember this day on which you went out of Egypt....no leavened bread shall be eaten...throughout the seven days matzot shall be eaten, nothing leavened, nor any leaven, shall be seen in your territory..."* Exodus 13:3,7

From these passages we learn that unique to the celebration of the holiday of Pesach is the eating of matzah, and the stringent prohibition of eating or possessing chometz. Chometz is a general term for all food and drink made from wheat, barley, rye, oats, spelt or their derivatives, which is leavened and thus forbidden on Pesach. Even a food that contains only a trace of chometz is prohibited and must be removed from our homes.

# How to Get Rid of Chometz

Obvious chometz — both food and utensils used throughout the year (and not "koshered" for Pesach) — should be stored in closets or rooms that are not easily accessible (locked or taped shut). This chometz should be sold to a non-Jew, as will be explained.

Clean the entire house thoroughly to remove all crumbs and small pieces of food. Also check for chometz in the car and office (desks and drawers, etc.), clothes, pockets (especially the children's), pocketbooks, attaché cases, and all other areas which may be easily overlooked. Vacuum cleaner bags should be discarded or cleaned.

# Shopping for Pesach

While shopping for Pesach we must be careful that the foods we buy are not only kosher but are also kosher-for-Pesach — that is, chometz-free. As an example, matzah used all year round is not necessarily kosher for Pesach use, only matzot baked especially for Pesach may be used on Pesach (check the label).

# Starting 'From Scratch'

All fresh fruits and vegetables as well as all kosher cuts of meat and kosher fish are all inherently kosher-for-Pesach. Of course, provided they have been prepared in accordance with Jewish law and have not come into contact with chometz or chometz utensils.

The prevailing [Ashkenazic] custom is that on Pesach we do not eat rice, millet, corn, mustard, legumes (beans, etc.) or foods made from them.

# Commercially Prepared Products

Nowadays, there are many kosher-for-Pesach packaged foods available. However, care must be used to purchase only those packaged foods that have a reliable Rabbinical supervision that is valid for Pesach.

Obviously, all leavened foods made from wheat, barley, rye, oats or spelt are actual chometz and are prohibited on Pesach. Examples are: bread, cake, cereal, spaghetti, beer and whiskey.

# Check that Medicine Cabinet!

Many medicines, sprays and cosmetics contain chometz. Consult a competent rabbi as to which ones may be used on Pesach. The same applies to pet food.

# Preparing the Kitchen

To prepare the kitchen for Pesach, we must "kosher" it from chometz that has been cooked in it.

### Dishes and Utensils:

Have special sets of dishes, silverware, pots, pans and other utensils for Pesach use only. (If necessary, certain year-round utensils may be used provided they are "koshered" for Pesach. To do so, consult a rabbi.)

### Stove:

Thoroughly clean and scour every part of it. Heat the oven to the highest temperature possible for 1-2 hours. Heat the grates and the iron parts of the stove (and elements if electric) until they glow red-hot. It is suggested that the oven and stove-top be covered afterwards with aluminum foil.

### Microwave Ovens:

Clean the oven thoroughly. Fill a completely clean container, that was not used for 24 hours, with water. Turn on the microwave and let it steam heavily. Turn it off and wipe out the inside. To use the microwave during Pesach, use a flat piece of Styrofoam or any other thick object as a separation between the bottom of the oven and the cooking dish. When cooking, the food should be covered on all sides.

### Sink:

Meticulously clean the sink. For 24 hours before "koshering" it, do not pour hot water from chometz pots into it. Afterwards, boil water in a clean pot that was not used for 24 hours, and pour it 3 times onto every part of the sink, including the drain stopper. Afterwards, line the sink.

*Refrigerator, Freezer, Cupboards, Closets, Tables and Counters:*

Thoroughly clean and scrub them to remove any crumbs and residue. Afterwards, cover those surfaces that come into contact with hot food or utensils with a heavy covering.

*Tablecloths and Napkins:*

Launder without starch.

# Selling Chometz

Since it is prohibited to possess chometz on Pesach, all chometz that we do not dispose of must be sold to a non-Jew for the duration of Pesach. This applies to all chometz that will not be eaten or burned before Pesach and all chometz utensils that will not be thoroughly cleaned by then. These are stored away in closets or rooms while preparing for Pesach. The storage area is locked or tape shut and they are leased to the non-Jew at the time of the sale.

Since there are many legal intricacies in this sale, only a competent rabbi should be entrusted with its execution. The rabbi acts as our agent both to sell the chometz to the non-Jew on the morning before Pesach starts and also to buy it back the evening after Pesach ends.

Remember that chometz which remains in the possession of a Jew over Pesach may not be used, eaten, bought or sold, after Pesach.

# Quick Shopping List for the Seder

In addition to preparing a sumptuous meal for our family and guests to be enjoyed during the meal portion of the seder, there are important items that are needed during the first part of the seder, in order to fulfill the complete mitzvah of the Pesach seder. These include (of course) the matzah, the bitter herbs, the *charoset*, etc..

As we will soon see, each of these items play a vital role during the unfolding of the seder.

So in addition to your standard festival-meal-for-family-and-guests shopping list, here are some items that you will need to get:

**Matzot** (for the seder plate) - Enough for everyone (3 p.p.).

**Wine** (for the four cups) - Enough for everyone (4 cups p.p.).

**Onions** (for *karpas*) - 1 large onion per 4 people (approx.).

**Chicken neck** (for *z'roa*) - 1 for each seder plate on the table.

**Cooked eggs** (for the *beitza*) - 1 for each seder plate on the table and p.p.

*Maror I* (for the *moror*) - Romaine lettuce (2-4 leaves p.p.)

*Maror II* (for the *moror*) - Horseradish root (4 ounces p.p.).

*Charoset* (for the *moror*) - Mixture of ground apples, pears, walnuts and wine. Small amount for each seder plate. (Usually homemade).

# *The Night Before Passover*

## The Search for Mr. Chometz

In the days and weeks leading to Pesach we begin cleaning our homes to rid chometz from our house and living areas. As the holiday draws near we need to make a formal, final search for any overlooked chometz. This is performed after nightfall on the 13th of Nissan (the night *before* the seder). This search for chometz is done with a lit candle, a feather (mini-broom), wooden spoon (mini-shovel), and a bag.

It is customary to place ten small pieces of bread, wrapped in paper or plastic, around the home before the search, so that the blessing over the search for chometz is not recited in vain.

After reciting the special blessing we hold the lit candle and the other "tools" as we search for chometz in every room, as well as any other area of the home and property that may have chometz, such as the basement, attic, garage or car.

As chometz is found it is swept into the bag and is burned (along with all remaining chometz) on the following morning.

# The Day Before Passover

## Fast of the Firstborn

During the tenth plague, when God slew the firstborn of Egypt, He spared the firstborn of the Children of Israel. Therefore, all firstborn sons of Israel, or fathers of firstborn sons under the age of 13, customarily fast on the day before Pesach, in gratitude to the Almighty for sparing them. It has, however, been a custom for many centuries that this fast day is broken by a *Siyum*, a festive meal in celebration of the conclusion of the study of a book of the Talmud. This usually takes place in the synagogue. Contact your local synagogue for the exact time.

## Burning of the Chometz

Any chometz that was found during the search for the chometz, or has not been eaten on the day before Pesach, is now burned.

We build a small fire near our residence in which the chometz is burned and consumed in the flames. This can easily be done in a metal pail, or small hand-made pit, etc.. Special blessings and prayers are recited, and we formally nullify all chometz in our possession.

Approximately one hour and fifteen minutes before the burning of the chometz we cease to eat any food that is not Kosher for Passover.

# *The Search for the Chometz*

The search for chometz is done after nightfall, on on the night of the 13th of Nissan (the night *before the seder*), with a beeswax candle, feather, and large wooden spoon, which is used to sweep all found chometz into a bag. It is customary to place ten small pieces of bread, wrapped in paper or plastic, around the home before the search, so that the blessing over the search for chometz is not recited in vain.

Recite the blessing below. Begin the search in the room closest to where the blessing was recited. Do not talk or interrupt the search until it is completed (unless the interruption is necessary for purposes of the search).

Böruch atöh adonöy, elohaynu    בָּרוּךְ אַתָּה יְהֹוָה אֱלֹהֵינוּ
melech hö-olöm, asher kid'shönu    מֶלֶךְ הָעוֹלָם, אֲשֶׁר קִדְּשָׁנוּ
b'mitzvosöv, v'tzivönu al    בְּמִצְוֹתָיו, וְצִוָּנוּ עַל
bi-ur chömaytz.    בְּעוּר חָמֵץ.

*Blessed are You, Lord our God, King of the universe, Who has sanctified us with His commandments and commanded us concerning the removal of chametz.*

Once you have completed the search in all corners, nooks, and crannies, and collected all the chometz together, recite the following:

Köl chamirö va-chami-ö d'ikö    כָּל חֲמִירָא וַחֲמִיעָא דְּאִכָּא
vir'shusi d'lö chamisay ud'lö    בִרְשׁוּתִי דְּלָא חֲמִיתֵיהּ וּדְלָא
vi-artay ud'lö y'da-nö lay li-bötayl    בְעַרְתֵּיהּ וּדְלָא יְדַעְנָא לֵיהּ לִבָּטֵל
v'le-hevay hefkayr k'afrö d'ar-ö.    וְלֶהֱוֵי הֶפְקֵר כְּעַפְרָא דְאַרְעָא:

*All leaven and leavened products that exist in my possession that I have not seen, have not removed, and do not know about, should be considered nullified and ownerless, like the dust of the earth.*

21

# The Burning of the Chometz

On the following morning, before the conclusion of the fifth hour from dawn (generally around 10-11 AM; check your calendar), a fire should be kindled in which the chometz found in the search and all remaining chometz in the house is burned. As the fire burns we recite the following declaration in which we nullify ownership of all chometz.

| | |
|---|---|
| Köl chamirö va-chami-ö d'ikö | כָּל חֲמִירָא וַחֲמִיעָא דְּאִכָּא |
| vir'shusi dacha-zisay ud'lö chazisay | בִּרְשׁוּתִי דַּחֲזִיתֵיהּ וּדְלָא חֲזִיתֵיהּ |
| da-chami-say ud'lö cha-misay, | דַּחֲמִיתֵיהּ וּדְלָא חֲמִיתֵיהּ |
| d'vi-artay ud'lö vi-artay li-bötayl | דְּבִעַרְתֵּיהּ וּדְלָא בִעַרְתֵּיהּ לִבְטַל |
| v'le-hevay hefkayr k'afrö d'ar-ö. | וְלֶהֱוֵי הֶפְקֵר כְּעַפְרָא דְאַרְעָא : |

*All leaven and leavened products that exist in my possession – whether I have seen it or have not seen it, whether I have observed it or have not observed it, whether I have removed it or have not removed it, should be considered nullified and ownerless, like the dust of the earth.*

| | |
|---|---|
| Y'hi rö-tzon mil'fönechö, adonöy | יְהִי רָצוֹן מִלְּפָנֶיךָ יְהֹוָה |
| elo-haynu vaylo-hay avo-saynu, | אֱלֹהֵינוּ וֵאלֹהֵי אֲבוֹתֵינוּ, |
| k'shaym she-ani m'va-ayr chömaytz | כְּשֵׁם שֶׁאֲנִי מְבַעֵר חָמֵץ |
| mibaysi umay-r'shusi kach t'va-ayr | מִבֵּיתִי וּמֵרְשׁוּתִי כַּךְ תְּבַעֵר |
| es köl ha-chi-tzonim v'es ru-ach | אֶת כָּל הַחִיצוֹנִים וְאֶת רוּחַ |
| ha-tum'öh ta-avir min hö-öretz | הַטּוּמְאָה תַּעֲבִיר מִן הָאָרֶץ |
| v'es yitz-raynu hö-rö ta-aviray-hu | וְאֶת יִצְרֵנוּ הָרָע תַּעֲבִירֵהוּ |

| | |
|---|---|
| may-itönu v'siten lönu layv bösör | מֵאִתָּנוּ וְתִתֵּן לָנוּ לֵב בָּשָׂר |
| l'öv-d'chö be-emes, v'chöl sitrö | לְעָבְדְּךָ בֶּאֱמֶת וְכָל סִטְרָא |
| öchörö v'chöl ha-k'lipos v'chöl | אָחֳרָא וְכָל הַקְּלִיפּוֹת וְכָל |
| hö-rish-öh be-öshön tichleh, v'sa-avir | הָרִשְׁעָה בֶּעָשָׁן תְּכַלֶּה וְתַעֲבִיר |
| memsheles zödon min hö-öretz, | מֶמְשֶׁלֶת זָדוֹן מִן הָאָרֶץ |
| v'chöl ha-m'ikim la-sh'chinöh | וְכָל הַמְּעִיקִים לַשְּׁכִינָה |
| t'va-araym b'ru-ach bö-ayr uv'ru-ach | תְּבַעֲרֵם בְּרוּחַ בָּעֵר וּבְרוּחַ |
| mishpöt, k'shaym she-bi-artö es | מִשְׁפָּט כְּשֵׁם שֶׁבִּעַרְתָּ אֶת |
| mitzra-yim v'es elohay-hem | מִצְרַיִם וְאֶת אֱלֹהֵיהֶם |
| ba-yömim hö-haym biz'man | בַּיָּמִים הָהֵם בִּזְמַן |
| ha-zeh, ömayn selöh. | הַזֶּה אָמֵן סֶלָה: |

*May it be Your will, Lord our God and God of our fathers, that just as I removed chametz from my home and possession, so too shall You remove all the chitzonim and cause the spirit of impurity to depart from the earth. Remove the evil inclination from us and grant us a heart of flesh to serve You with truth. Abolish all the sitra achara, all kelipot, and consume all wickedness in smoke, and remove the dominion of defiance from the earth. And all those that distress the Shechinah remove with a spirit of destruction and a spirit of judgment, just as You destroyed Egypt and its gods in those days at this time. Amen. Selah.*

23

# Seder Preparations

## A Royal Feast

On the first two nights of Pesach we conduct a seder — a festive yet solemn event. At a table royally set with our best crystal and silver and the finest of kosher red wines, we reenact the exodus from Egypt in ancient times. We also pray for the forthcoming redemption speedily in our days.

## In Our Forefathers' Footsteps

At the seder, each person considers himself as if he were going out of Egypt. We begin with our ancestors, Abraham, Isaac and Jacob; we follow the plight of our people as they descend into exile and suffer cruel oppression and persecution. We are with them when God sends the ten plagues to punish Pharaoh and his nation, then we join them as they leave Egypt and as they cross the Reed Sea. We witness the miraculous hand of God as the waters part, allowing the Israelites to pass, and then return, thundering over the Egyptian legions.

## Matzah, The "Food of Faith"

We left Egypt in such haste that there was no time to wait for the dough to rise, therefore we ate matzah, unleavened bread. With only this unleavened food as their provisions at the Exodus, our ancestors went into the desert, faithfully relying on the Almighty to provide sustenance for an entire nation of men, women and children. Each year to remember this, we eat matzah the first two nights of Pesach and fulfill the commandment of "Matzot shall you eat ..."

The matzah itself symbolizes faith. For in contrast to leavened food, the matzah is not "enriched" with oil, honey, etc. It is rather simple flour and water, which is not allowed to rise. Similarly, the only "ingredients" for faith are humility and submission to God, which comes from the realization of our "nothingness" and "intellectual poverty" in the face of the infinite wisdom of the creator.

## *Shmurah* Matzah

*Shmurah* means watched or guarded, and is an apt description of this matzah (unleavened bread). The wheat used is carefully watched (protected) against any contact with water from the moment of harvest, since water causes leavening, and thus disqualify the wheat for use on Pesach.

These matzot are round in shape, kneaded and formed by hand, similar to the matzot baked by the Children of Israel on their way out of Egypt. The matzot are baked under strict rabbinical supervision to avoid any possibility of leavening during the baking process. *Shmurah* matzah should be used on each of the two seder nights for the three matzot of the seder plate.

# Seder Basics

The Pesach seder is not to be observed just symbolically. Each of its physical "acts" has a profound significance and should be fulfilled properly to make the seder a meaningful and truly spiritual experience.

## The Main Mitzvot

The main mitzvot (commandments) of the seder are:

1. To eat matzah.

2. To tell the story of the Exodus (the recital of the main parts of the Haggadah).

3. To drink four cups of wine.

4. To eat *moror* - bitter herbs.

5. To recite "*Hallel*" praise to God.

## The Matzah

Matzah is eaten 3 times during the seder.

1. After telling the story of the Exodus from Egypt — *Motzi Matzah* — those with a traditional seder plate eats two ounces, and everyone else eats one ounce.

2. For the "sandwich" — *korech* — 0.75 ounce of matzah is eaten.

3. Finally for the *Afikoman* at the end of the meal — *Tzofun* — one ounce of matzah are eaten. Some eat two ounces.

In each instance, the matzah should be eaten within four minutes. A half a piece of hand-made *shmurah* matzah is generally one ounce. If other matzot are used, the weight of the box of matzot divided by the number of pieces shows how much matzah equals one ounce.

Note: Matzah made from flour kneaded with fruit juice or eggs (egg matzah) should not be used for the seder (except by the elderly or sick who cannot digest regular matzah).

# The Wine

For each of the four cups at the seder it is preferable to use undiluted wine. However, if needed, the wine may be diluted with grape juice. Of course, someone who can not drink wine (children, the elderly and infirm) may use pure grape juice.

Two of the explanations for why we drink four cups is:

a) alluding to the Four expressions of freedom and deliverance mentioned in the Torah in connection with our liberation from Egypt (Exodus 6:6,7).

b) The Children of Israel, even while in Egyptian exile, had four great merits: 1) They did not change their Hebrew names. 2) They did not change their Hebrew language. 3) They remained highly moral. 4) They remained loyal to one another.

We drink a cup of wine (at least 3.5 ounces) four times during the seder:

1. At the conclusion of *Kiddush*.

2. After telling the story of the Exodus from Egypt, before eating the matzah of *Motzi Matzah*.

3. At the conclusion of the Grace After Meals.

4. After reciting the "*Hallel*."

It is preferable to drink the entire cup each time. However, it is sufficient to drink just the majority of each cup.

## The *Moror* (Bitter Herbs)

The *moror* is eaten by itself, after the eating of the matzah, and then together with matzah in the *koreich* "sandwich." In each instance at least 0.75 of an ounce should be eaten.

Any of two different types of *moror* may be used at the seder:

1. Peeled and grated raw horseradish. 0.75 ounce has a volume of 1 fluid ounce.

2. Romaine lettuce. One regular size leaf is usually 0.75 of an ounce.

# How to Prepare the Seder Plate

Three matzot are placed on a plate or decorated tray, one on top of the other. They are symbolic of the three types of Jews: *Kohen*, *Levi* and *Yisroel*. They also commemorate the three measures of fine flour that Abraham told Sarah to bake into matzot when the three angels visited them. And when we later break the middle matzah, we are still left with two whole loaves for *lechem mishne*, as on all Sabbaths and Festivals.

On a cloth spread over the three matzot, or on a plate, the following items are placed:

**1. *"Z'roa"* — The roasted chicken neck.**

Preparation: remove most of the meat from the neck of a chicken and roast it on all sides. It is symbolic of the Paschal sacrifice brought at the Holy Temple in Jerusalem on the afternoon before Pesach.

**2. *"Baytzah"* — The hard boiled egg.**

It is symbolic of the festival sacrifice brought at the Holy Temple, in addition to the Paschal lamb.

**3. *"Moror"* — The bitter herbs (Horseradish root).**

It is symbolic of the bitter suffering of the Jews in Egypt.

**4. *"Charoset"* — Mixture of chopped apples, pears, walnuts and wine.**

31

The mixture resembles mortar, symbolic of the mortar used by the Israelites to make bricks while enslaved in Egypt.

5. *"Karpas"* — Some raw onion or cooked potato.
   Used near the beginning of the seder.

6. *"Chazeret"* — bitter herbs (romaine lettuce stalks).
   Used as *moror* and in the sandwich (*koreich*) later in the seder.

**Below is a diagram of how the items
are placed on the seder plate:**

# *The Order of The Seder*

## *Kadeish*
## The Benediction

The seder service begins with the recitation of *Kiddush*, proclaiming the holiness of the holiday. This is done over a cup of wine, and on this evening it is the first of four cups that we all drink, reclining, at the seder. Wine is used because it is a symbol of joy and happiness. When drinking the four cups, as during most of the acts of the seder, we recline on our left side, a sign of royalty, to accentuate the fact that we are a free people. In ancient times only free people were allowed to recline during meals.

## *Ur'chatz*
## Purification

We wash our hands in the usual prescribed manner of washing before a meal, but without the customary blessing. The next step in the seder, *Karpas*, requires dipping food into water. Such an act calls for purification of the hands by washing beforehand. This observance is one of the first acts designed to arouse the child's curiosity.

## *Karpas*
# The Appetizer

A small piece of onion or cooked potato is dipped into salt water and eaten. Before eating, the blessing over vegetables is recited.

The dipping of this appetizer in salt water is an act of pleasure and freedom, and further arouses the curiosity of the child. Also, the four-letter Hebrew word *karpas,* when read backwards, connotes that the 600,000 Jews in Egypt (the Hebrew letter *samach* equals sixty times 10,000) were forced to perform back-breaking labor (the other three Hebrew letters spell *perech* – hard work). The salt water represents the tears of our ancestors in Egypt.

## *Yachatz*
# Breaking the Matzah

The middle matzah of the three placed on the seder plate is broken in two. The larger part is put aside for use later as the *Afikoman.* This unusual action not only attracts the child's special attention once again, but also recalls God's breaking the Reed Sea asunder, to make a path for the Children of Israel to cross on dry land.

The smaller part of the middle matzah is returned to the seder plate. This broken middle matzah symbolizes humility and will be alluded to in the next stage as the "bread of poverty."

# *Maggid*
# The Haggadah

At this point the poor are invited to join the seder; the seder plate is moved aside; a second cup of wine is poured; and the child, by now bursting with curiosity, asks the four time-honored questions.

The child's questioning triggers one of the most significant mitzvot of Pesach and the highlight of the seder ceremony: the Haggadah, the telling of the story of the exodus from Egypt.

The answer includes a brief review of history, a description of the suffering imposed upon the Israelites, a listing of the plagues visited upon the Egyptians, and an enumeration of the miracles performed by the Almighty for the formation and redemption of His people.

# *Rochtzoh*
# Washing before the Meal

After reciting the first part of the Haggadah and drinking of the second cup of wine, we wash our hands in the ritual manner – this time reciting the customary blessing, as usually done before eating bread.

## *Motzi Matzah*
## Eating Matzah

The three matzot are held, the broken one between the two whole ones, and the customary blessing for bread is recited. Then, the bottom matzah is allowed to drop back onto the plate, and holding the top whole matzah with the broken middle one, a special blessing for the mitzvah of eating matzah is recited.

For those with a traditional seder plate, one ounce from each matzah is broken off (others just one ounce), the two pieces are eaten together, while reclining to the left.

## *Moror*
## The Bitter Herbs

At least 0.75 of an ounce of the bitter herbs are taken and dipped into the *charoset*, and the special blessing for the mitzvah of eating *maror* is recited. We also have in mind the *Koreich* sandwich (below). The *moror* is eaten without reclining.

## *Koreich*
## The Sandwich

In keeping with the custom instituted by Hillel, a great Talmudic rabbi, a sandwich of matzah and *moror* is made. We break off two pieces of the bottom matzah, which together should amount to at least one ounce.

36

We also take at least 0.75 of an ounce of bitter herbs and dip them into the *charoset* (we then shake of some of the *charoset* so as not to dilute the bitter taste), then place them in between the two pieces of matzah. We then recite a special passage explaining this practice and eat the sandwich while reclining.

## *Shulchon Oraych*
## The Feast

The holiday meal is served. We begin the meal with a hard-boiled egg dipped into salt water. A rabbi was once asked why Jews eat an egg at the seder. "Because eggs symbolize the Jew," the rabbi answered, "The more an egg is boiled, the harder it gets."

Note: The *z'roa* (shankbone or chicken neck) is not eaten at the seder, nor should any other roast meat be served, so as not to make it appear that we are eating the Paschal sacrifice (which could only be offered in the Holy Temple).

## *Tzofun*
## The Hidden *Afikoman*

After the meal, the half matzah that had been "hidden" — set aside for the *Afikoman* — "dessert," is taken out and eaten. It symbolizes the Paschal lamb that was eaten at the end of the meal in Temple times together with the matzah.

Everyone eats at least one ounce of matzah while reclining. Some have the custom to eat two ounces. This is done before midnight. After the *Afikoman* we do not eat or drink anything, except for the two remaining cups of wine.

## *Bairach*
## Grace After the Meal

A third cup of wine, and the Cup of Elijah is filled, and the Grace After Meals is recited. After reciting the Grace, we recite the blessing on wine and drink the third cup while reclining.

We then open the door, which symbolizes an invitation to the Prophet Elijah, who is the harbinger of the coming of *Moshiach*, our righteous redeemer. We then recite the passage that expresses our yearning for the redemption.

## *Hallel*
## Songs of Praise

At this point, having recognized the Almighty and His unique guidance of His people Israel, we go still further and turn to sing His praises as Lord of the entire Universe. After reciting the "*Hallel*" (Verses of Praise), we again recite the blessing for wine and drink the fourth cup, reclining.

# *Nirtzoh*
## Acceptance

Having carried out the seder service properly, we are sure that it has been well received by the Almighty.

# Candle Lighting

On Pesach, as on the Shabbat and festivals throughout the year, Jewish women and girls are granted the privilege and the responsibility of lighting the candles to usher in the holiness of the holiday into the home. The holiday candles should be lit at least 18 minutes before sunset. Unlike candle lighting on the Shabbat, however, if the candles are not lit before sunset, they may be lit afterwards. In such a situation, however, the candles must be lit from an existing flame (i.e. stove burner, 24-hour candle, etc.), since it is forbidden to create a new fire on the holiday.

On the second night of Pesach, the candles are lit from an existing flame after the appearance of three stars (about 72 mintues after sunset).

When the first day of Pesach falls on the Shabbat, candle lighting for the 2nd day is delayed until the appearance of three stars. Before lighting the candles, one should recite the phrase, "*Baruch hamavdil bein kodesh lekodesh*" — "Blessed is He Who made a distinction between the holy and the holy." Here too, the candles are lit from an existing flame.

For the seventh and eighth days of Pesach, the procedure is the same as for the first and second days, except that on these two days the blessing "*Shehecheyanu*" — "Who has granted us life..." — is not recited.

# *Blessings for Candle Lighting*

At the appropriate time (see local Jewish calendar) light the candle(s). Draw your hands three times around the candle(s) and toward your face. Cover your eyes with your hands and recite the following two blessings.

### For the Eve of Passover that falls on a Weekday

Böruch atöh adonöy, elohaynu     בָּרוּךְ אַתָּה יְהֹוָה, אֱלֹהֵינוּ

melech hö-olöm, asher kid'shönu     מֶלֶךְ הָעוֹלָם, אֲשֶׁר קִדְּשָׁנוּ

b'mitzvosöv, v'tzivönu l'hadlik     בְּמִצְוֹתָיו, וְצִוָּנוּ לְהַדְלִיק

nayr shel yom tov.     נֵר שֶׁל יוֹם טוֹב:

*Blessed are You, Lord our God, King of the universe, Who has sanctified us with His commandments, and commanded us to kindle the Yom Tov light.*

### Continue with:

Böruch atöh adonöy, elohaynu,     בָּרוּךְ אַתָּה יְהֹוָה, אֱלֹהֵינוּ,

melech hö-olöm, she-heche-yönu     מֶלֶךְ הָעוֹלָם, שֶׁהֶחֱיָנוּ

v'kiy'mönu v'higi-önu liz'man ha-zeh     וְקִיְּמָנוּ וְהִגִּיעָנוּ לִזְמַן הַזֶּה:

*Blessed are You, Lord our God, King of the universe, Who has granted us life, sustained us and enabled us to reach this occasion.*

### For the Eve of Shabbat and Passover

Böruch atöh adonöy, elohaynu     בָּרוּךְ אַתָּה יְהֹוָה, אֱלֹהֵינוּ מֶלֶךְ

melech hö-olöm, asher kid'shönu     הָעוֹלָם, אֲשֶׁר קִדְּשָׁנוּ

b'mitzvosöv, v'tzivönu l'hadlik     בְּמִצְוֹתָיו, וְצִוָּנוּ לְהַדְלִיק

nayr shel shabös v'shel yom tov.     נֵר שֶׁל שַׁבָּת וְשֶׁל יוֹם טוֹב:

*Blessed are You, Lord our God, King of the universe, Who has sanctified us with His commandments, and commanded us to kindle the Shabbat and Yom Tov light.*

**Continue with:**

Böruch atöh adonöy, elohaynu בָּרוּךְ אַתָּה יְהוָֹה, אֱלֹהֵינוּ
melech hö-olöm, she-heche-yönu מֶלֶךְ הָעוֹלָם, שֶׁהֶחֱיָנוּ
v'kiy'mönu v'higi-önu liz'man ha-zeh. וְקִיְּמָנוּ וְהִגִּיעָנוּ לִזְמַן הַזֶּה:

*Blessed are You, Lord our God, King of the universe, Who has granted us life, sustained us and enabled us to reach this occasion.*

# *The Seder Begins*

After the family gathers around the table and the seder plates have been assembled, we begin with a review of the "Order of the Seder."

| | |
|---|---|
| Kadaysh. Ur'chatz. Karpas. Yachatz. | קַדֵּשׁ. וּרְחַץ. כַּרְפַּס. יַחַץ. |
| Magid. Röchtzö. Motzi Matzöh. | מַגִּיד. רָחְצָה. מוֹצִיא מַצָּה. |
| Möror. Koraych. Shulchön Oraych. | מָרוֹר. כּוֹרֵךְ. שֻׁלְחָן עוֹרֵךְ. |
| Tzöfun. Bay-rach. Halayl. Nirtzöh. | צָפוּן. בֵּרַךְ. הַלֵּל. נִרְצָה: |

*Reciting the Kiddush. Washing the hands. Eating a vegetable dipped in salt-water. Breaking the middle matzah. Reciting the Haggadah. Washing the hands a second time. The blessing "Hamotzi." Eating the matzah. Eating the bitter herbs. Eating a sandwich of matzah and bitter herbs. Eating the festive meal. Eating the Afikoman. Reciting Grace After a Meal. Reciting psalms of praise. The seder is favorably accepted.*

---

## • *Kadeish* •
## The Benediction

---

The seder begins with the recitation of *Kiddush* by everyone, proclaiming the holiness of the holiday. This is done over a cup of wine. Wine is used because it is a symbol of joy and happiness. When drinking any of the "Four Cups" we lean to our left in the manner of kings, to accentuate the fact that we are a free people.

Askinu s'udöso d'mal'kö i-lö-öh    אַתְקִינוּ סְעוּדָתָא דְמַלְכָּא עִלָּאָה

dö hi s'udö-sö d'kud-shö    דָּא הִיא סְעוּדָתָא דְקוּדְשָׁא

b'rich hu ush'chintay.    בְּרִיךְ הוּא וּשְׁכִינְתֵּיהּ :

*Prepare the meal of the supernal King. This is the meal of the Holy One, blessed be He, and His Shechinah.*

The Kiddush is recited standing, with a cup of wine containing at least 3.5 fluid ounces. Lift the cup with your right hand. Transfer it to the left hand. Lower it into the cupped palm of your right hand (if you write with your left hand, reverse). Lift the cup at least 3 inches above the table. Recite the blessings below.

On Shabbat begin here:

Yom ha-shishi. Va-y'chulu    יוֹם הַשִּׁשִּׁי : וַיְכֻלּוּ

hashöma-yim v'hö-öretz v'chöl    הַשָּׁמַיִם וְהָאָרֶץ וְכָל

tz'vö-öm. Va-y'chal elohim ba-yom    צְבָאָם : וַיְכַל אֱלֹהִים בַּיּוֹם

ha-sh'vi-i, m'lachto asher ösöh,    הַשְּׁבִיעִי, מְלַאכְתּוֹ אֲשֶׁר עָשָׂה,

va-yishbos ba-yom ha-sh'vi-i miköl    וַיִּשְׁבֹּת בַּיּוֹם הַשְּׁבִיעִי מִכָּל

m'lachto asher ösöh. Va-y'vörech    מְלַאכְתּוֹ אֲשֶׁר עָשָׂה : וַיְבָרֶךְ

elohim es yom ha-sh'vi-i,    אֱלֹהִים אֶת יוֹם הַשְּׁבִיעִי,

va-y'kadaysh oso, ki vo shövas    וַיְקַדֵּשׁ אֹתוֹ, כִּי בוֹ שָׁבַת

miköl m'lachto, asher börö    מִכָּל מְלַאכְתּוֹ, אֲשֶׁר בָּרָא

elohim la-asos.    אֱלֹהִים לַעֲשׂוֹת :

*The sixth day. And the heavens and the earth and all their hosts were completed. And God finished by the Seventh Day His work which He had done, and He rested on the Seventh Day from all His work which He had done. And God blessed the Seventh Day and made it holy, for on it He rested from all His work which God created to function.*

**On Shabbat continue here (include all parenthasized words).**
**During the week begin here:**

Savri mörönön: Böruch atöh adonöy
elohaynu melech hö-olöm,
boray p'ri ha-göfen.

סַבְרִי מָרָנָן : בָּרוּךְ אַתָּה יְהֹוָה
אֱלֹהֵינוּ מֶלֶךְ הָעוֹלָם,
בּוֹרֵא פְּרִי הַגָּפֶן :

*Attention, gentlemen! Blessed are You, Lord our God, King of the universe, Who creates the fruit of the vine.*

Böruch atöh adonöy elohaynu
melech hö-olöm, asher böchar bönu
miköl öm v'ro-m'mönu miköl löshon
v'kid'shönu b'mitzvosöv, vatiten
lönu adonöy elohaynu b'ahavöh
(shabösos lim'nuchöh u-)
mo-adim l'simchöh chagim
uz'manim l'söson, es yom
(ha-shabös ha-zeh v'es yom)
chag ha-matzos ha-zeh, v'es yom tov
mikrö kodesh ha-zeh,
z'man chayrusaynu
(b'ahavöh) mikrö kodesh zaycher

בָּרוּךְ אַתָּה יְהֹוָה אֱלֹהֵינוּ
מֶלֶךְ הָעוֹלָם, אֲשֶׁר בָּחַר בָּנוּ
מִכָּל עָם וְרוֹמְמָנוּ מִכָּל לָשׁוֹן
וְקִדְּשָׁנוּ בְּמִצְוֹתָיו, וַתִּתֶּן
לָנוּ יְהֹוָה אֱלֹהֵינוּ בְּאַהֲבָה
(שַׁבָּתוֹת לִמְנוּחָה וּ)
מוֹעֲדִים לְשִׂמְחָה חַגִּים
וּזְמַנִּים לְשָׂשׂוֹן אֶת יוֹם
(הַשַּׁבָּת הַזֶּה וְאֶת יוֹם)
חַג הַמַּצּוֹת הַזֶּה וְאֶת יוֹם טוֹב
מִקְרָא קֹדֶשׁ הַזֶּה,
זְמַן חֵרוּתֵנוּ
(בְּאַהֲבָה) מִקְרָא קֹדֶשׁ זֵכֶר

46

li-tzi-as mitzrö-yim, ki vönu     לִיצִיאַת מִצְרַיִם, כִּי בָנוּ

vöchartö v'osönu kidashtö miköl     בָחַרְתָּ וְאוֹתָנוּ קִדַּשְׁתָּ מִכָּל

hö-amim, (v'shabös) umo-aday     הָעַמִּים, (וְשַׁבָּת) וּמוֹעֲדֵי

ködshechö (b'ahavöh uvrötzon)     קָדְשֶׁךָ (בְּאַהֲבָה וּבְרָצוֹן)

b'simchöh uv'söson hin-chaltönu.     בְּשִׂמְחָה וּבְשָׂשׂוֹן הִנְחַלְתָּנוּ:

Böruch atöh adonöy     בָּרוּךְ אַתָּה יְיָ

m'kadaysh (hashabbös v')     מְקַדֵּשׁ (הַשַּׁבָּת וְ)

yisrö-ayl v'haz'manim.     יִשְׂרָאֵל וְהַזְּמַנִּים:

**On Saturday night, continue with Havdalah on page 48.**
**Otherwise continue below (women do not recite this blessing on the 2nd night):**

Böruch atöh adonöy, elohaynu     בָּרוּךְ אַתָּה יְהֹוָה אֱלֹהֵינוּ

melech hö-olöm, she-heche-yönu     מֶלֶךְ הָעוֹלָם, שֶׁהֶחֱיָנוּ

v'kiy'mönu v'higi-önu     וְקִיְּמָנוּ וְהִגִּיעָנוּ

liz'man ha-zeh.     לִזְמַן הַזֶּה:

*Blessed are You, Lord our God, King of the universe, Who has chosen us from among all nations, raised us above all tongues, and made us holy through His commandments. And You, Lord our God, have given us in love (on Shabbat: Sabbaths for rest and) Festivals for rejoicing, holidays and seasons for gladness, (on Shabbat: this Shabbat day and) this day of the Festival of Matzot, and this Festival of holy assembly, the season of our freedom (on Shabbat: in love), a holy convocation, commemorating the departure from Egypt. For You have chosen us and sanctified us from all the nations, and You have given us as a heritage Your holy (on Shabbat: Shabbat and) Festivals (on Shabbat: in love and favor), in happiness and joy. Blessed are You, Lord, Who sanctifies (on Shabbat: the Shabbos and) Israel and the [festive]* seasons. Blessed are You, Lord our God, King of the universe, Who has granted us life, sustained us and enabled us to reach this occasion.

**Sit down, and drink the wine (at least 2 ounces), reclining to the left.**

---

### Havdalah for when the Festival falls on Saturday night:

**Recited on a flame:** Böruch atöh adonöy elohaynu melech hö-olöm, boray m'oray hö-aysh. **Look at the flame.**

בָּרוּךְ אַתָּה יְהֹוָה אֱלֹהֵינוּ מֶלֶךְ הָעוֹלָם, בּוֹרֵא מְאוֹרֵי הָאֵשׁ.

Böruch atöh adonöy elohaynu melech hö-olöm, ha-mavdil bayn kodesh l'chol, bayn or l'choshech, bayn yisrö-ayl lö-amim, bayn yom ha-sh'vi-i l'shayshes y'may hama-aseh. Bayn k'dushas shabös lik'dushas yom tov hivdaltö, v'es yom ha-sh'vi-i mi-shayshes y'may ha-ma-aseh kidashtö, hivdaltö v'kidashtö es am'chö yisrö-ayl bik'dushösechö. Böruch atöh adonöy, ha-mavdil bayn kodesh l'kodesh.

בָּרוּךְ אַתָּה יְהֹוָה אֱלֹהֵינוּ מֶלֶךְ הָעוֹלָם, הַמַּבְדִּיל בֵּין קֹדֶשׁ לְחוֹל, בֵּין אוֹר לְחֹשֶׁךְ, בֵּין יִשְׂרָאֵל לָעַמִּים, בֵּין יוֹם הַשְּׁבִיעִי לְשֵׁשֶׁת יְמֵי הַמַּעֲשֶׂה. בֵּין קְדֻשַּׁת שַׁבָּת לִקְדֻשַּׁת יוֹם טוֹב הִבְדַּלְתָּ, וְאֶת יוֹם הַשְּׁבִיעִי מִשֵּׁשֶׁת יְמֵי הַמַּעֲשֶׂה קִדַּשְׁתָּ, הִבְדַּלְתָּ וְקִדַּשְׁתָּ אֶת עַמְּךָ יִשְׂרָאֵל בִּקְדֻשָּׁתֶךָ. בָּרוּךְ אַתָּה יְיָ, הַמַּבְדִּיל בֵּין קֹדֶשׁ לְקֹדֶשׁ:

Böruch atöh adonöy, elohaynu melech hö-olöm, she-heche-yönu

בָּרוּךְ אַתָּה יְהֹוָה אֱלֹהֵינוּ מֶלֶךְ הָעוֹלָם, שֶׁהֶחֱיָנוּ

48

v'kiy'mönu v'higi-önu  וְקִיְּמָנוּ וְהִגִּיעָנוּ

liz'man ha-zeh.  לִזְמַן הַזֶּה :

*Blessed are You, Lord our God, King of the universe, Who creates the lights of fire. Blessed are You, Lord our God, King of the universe, Who makes a distinction between sacred and profane, between light and darkness, between Israel and the nations, between the Seventh Day and the six work days; between the holiness of the Shabbat and the holiness of the Festival You have made a distinction, and have sanctified the Seventh Day above the six work days. You have set apart and made holy Your people Israel with Your holiness. Blessed are You Lord, Who makes a distinction between holy and holy. Blessed are You, Lord our God, King of the universe, Who has granted us life, sustained us and enabled us to reach this occasion.*

Sit down, and drink the wine (at least 2 ounces), reclining to the left.

# • *Urchatz* •
## Washing the Hands

Everyone washes the hands in the usual prescribed manner of washing before a meal but without the customary blessing. This observance is one of the first acts designed to arouse the child's curiosity.

Remove any rings. Fill a large cup with at least 3.5 ounces of cold water, while holding it in your right hand. Transfer the cup to your left hand and pour three times over your whole right hand. Transfer it to your right hand and pour three times over your whole left hand. Rub your hands together. Dry your hands and do not make a blessing.

# • *Karpas* •
## Eating a Vegetable Dipped in Salt Water

A small piece of onion or boiled potato is dipped into salt water and eaten. Before eating, the blessing over vegetables is recited.

The dipping of this appetizer in salt water is an act of pleasure and freedom which further arouses the curiosity of the child. The four-letter Hebrew word *karpas*, when read backwards, alludes to the

600,000 Jews in Egypt (the Hebrew letter *samech*=60, times 10,000) were forced to perform back-breaking labor (the other three Hebrew letters spell *perech* — hard work). The salt water represents the tears of our ancestors in Egypt.

Take a small piece of karpas (less than the size of an olive) and dip it into salt water. When reciting the blessing below have in mind that the blessing is also for the bitter herbs that will be eaten later. The karpas is eaten without reclining. The remaining karpas is not returned to the seder plate.

Böruch atöh adonöy elohaynu    בָּרוּךְ אַתָּה יְהֹוָה אֱלֹהֵינוּ

melech hö-olöm, boray    מֶלֶךְ הָעוֹלָם בּוֹרֵא

pri hö-adömö.    פְּרִי הָאֲדָמָה:

*Blessed are You, Lord our God, King of the universe, Who created the fruit of the earth.*

---

## • *Yachatz* •
## Breaking the Middle Matzah

---

The middle matzah of the three placed on the seder plate is broken in two. The larger part is put aside for use later as the *Afikoman*. This unusual action not only attracts the child's special attention once again, but also recalls God's breaking the Reed Sea asunder, to make a path for the Children of Israel to cross on dry land. The smaller part of the middle matzah is returned to the seder plate. This broken middle matzah symbolizes humility and will be alluded to in the next stage as the "bread of poverty."

51

Hold the middle matzah while it is still under its covering and break it in two. The larger half is set aside for the *Afikoman*. The smaller half is left between the two remaining matzot. It is customary to break the bigger half (the *Afikoman*) into five pieces and wrap it in a cloth or napkin. The *Afikoman* is put aside until after the meal.

---

## • *Maggid* •
### Reciting the Haggadah

---

Before we begin retelling the story of the Exodus, we declare that the poor of our community are invited to join our seder. Then the second cup of wine is poured and the four questions are asked.

The child's questioning triggers one of the most significant mitzvot of Pesach and the highlight of the seder ceremony: the Haggadah, the telling of the story of the exodus from Egypt. The answer includes a brief review of history, a description of the suffering imposed upon the Israelites, a listing of the plagues visited upon the Egyptians, and an enumeration of the miracles performed by the Almighty for the redemption of His people.

Uncover the matzot partially and recite the following passage:

| | |
|---|---|
| Hay lach-mö anyö di achölu | הָא לַחְמָא עַנְיָא דִי אֲכָלוּ |
| av-hösönö b'a-röh d'mitzrö-yim. Kol | אַבְהָתָנָא בְּאַרְעָא דְמִצְרָיִם. כֹּל |
| dich'fin yaysay v'yaychol. Kol ditzrich | דִּכְפִין יֵיתֵי וְיֵיכוֹל. כֹּל דִּצְרִיךְ |
| yaysay v'yifsöch. Ha-shatöh höchö. | יֵיתֵי וְיִפְסַח. הַשַּׁתָּא הָכָא. |

L'shönöh ha-bö-öh b'ar-ö d'yisrö-ayl. לְשָׁנָה הַבָּאָה בְּאַרְעָא דְיִשְׂרָאֵל.
Ha-shatö avdin l'shönöh הַשַׁתָּא עַבְדִּין לְשָׁנָה
ha-bö-öh b'nay chorin. הַבָּאָה בְּנֵי חוֹרִין:

*This is the bread of affliction that our fathers ate in the land of Egypt. Whoever is hungry, let him come and eat. Whoever is in need, let him come and join in celebrating the Pesach Festival. This year [we are] here; next year, in Eretz Yisrael. This year we are slaves; next year free men.*

# The Four Questions

Cover the Matzot. The second cup of wine is filled. It is customary that all the children recite the Four Questions. After the last child finishes reciting the questions, the person leading the seder repeats the Four Questions, followed by all present.

1. Mah nishtanöh ha-lai-y'löh מַה נִּשְׁתַּנָּה הַלַּיְלָה .1
ha-zeh miköl ha-laylos. הַזֶּה מִכָּל הַלֵּילוֹת:
Sheb'chöl ha-laylos ayn önu שֶׁבְּכָל הַלֵּילוֹת אֵין אָנוּ
mat-bilin afilu pa-am echös, מַטְבִּילִין אֲפִילוּ פַּעַם אֶחָת,
ha-lai-y'löh ha-zeh shtay f'ömim. הַלַּיְלָה הַזֶּה שְׁתֵּי פְעָמִים:

2. Sheb'chöl ha-laylos önu och'lin שֶׁבְּכָל הַלֵּילוֹת אָנוּ אוֹכְלִין .2
chömaytz o matzöh, ha-lai-y'löh ha-zeh חָמֵץ אוֹ מַצָּה, הַלַּיְלָה הַזֶּה
kulo matzöh. כֻּלּוֹ מַצָּה:

3. Sheb'chöl ha-laylos önu och'lin sh'ör שֶׁבְּכָל הַלֵּילוֹת אָנוּ אוֹכְלִין שְׁאָר .3
y'rökos, ha-lai-y'löh ha-zeh möror. יְרָקוֹת, הַלַּיְלָה הַזֶּה מָרוֹר:

4. Sheb'chöl ha-laylos önu och'lin
bayn yosh'vin uvayn m'subin,
ha-lai-y'löh ha-zeh kulönu m'subin.

שֶׁבְּכָל הַלֵּילוֹת אָנוּ אוֹכְלִין 4.
בֵּין יוֹשְׁבִין וּבֵין מְסֻבִּין,
הַלַּיְלָה הַזֶּה כֻּלָּנוּ מְסֻבִּין:

*Why is this night different from all other nights? 1. On all other nights, we do not dip even once, but on this night we dip twice. 2. On all other nights, we eat chometz (leavened bread) or matzah, but on this night, only matzah. 3. On all other nights, we eat any type of vegetables, but on this night we eat maror. 4. On all other nights, we eat either sitting upright or reclining, but on this night we all recline.*

Uncover the matzot partially. The story of the Haggadah is recounted out loud, and with joy.

Avödim hö-yinu l'far-oh b'mitzrö-yim
va-yo-tzi-aynu adonöy elohaynu
mishöm b'yöd chazököh uviz'ro-ah
n'tu-yöh. V'ilu lo ho-tzi ha-ködosh
böruch hu es avosaynu mimi-tzra-yim
haray önu uvönaynu uv'nay vönaynu
m'shu-bödim höyinu l'far-oh
b'mitzrö-yim. Va-afilu kulönu
chachö-mim kulönu n'vonim kulönu
yo-d'im es ha-toröh mitzvöh ölaynu
l'sapayr bi-tzi-as mitzrö-yim. V'chöl
ha-marbeh l'sapayr bi-tzi-as
mitzra-yim haray zeh m'shuböch.

עֲבָדִים הָיִינוּ לְפַרְעֹה בְּמִצְרַיִם
וַיּוֹצִיאֵנוּ יְהֹוָה אֱלֹהֵינוּ
מִשָּׁם בְּיָד חֲזָקָה וּבִזְרוֹעַ
נְטוּיָה. וְאִלּוּ לֹא הוֹצִיא הַקָּדוֹשׁ
בָּרוּךְ הוּא אֶת אֲבוֹתֵינוּ מִמִּצְרַיִם
הֲרֵי אָנוּ וּבָנֵינוּ וּבְנֵי בָנֵינוּ
מְשֻׁעְבָּדִים הָיִינוּ לְפַרְעֹה
בְּמִצְרָיִם. וַאֲפִילוּ כֻּלָּנוּ
חֲכָמִים כֻּלָּנוּ נְבוֹנִים כֻּלָּנוּ
יוֹדְעִים אֶת הַתּוֹרָה מִצְוָה עָלֵינוּ
לְסַפֵּר בִּיצִיאַת מִצְרָיִם. וְכָל
הַמַּרְבֶּה לְסַפֵּר בִּיצִיאַת
מִצְרַיִם הֲרֵי זֶה מְשֻׁבָּח:

*We were slaves to Pharaoh in Egypt, and the Lord our God took us out from there with a strong hand and an outstretched arm. Had the Holy One, blessed be He, not taken our fathers out of Egypt, then we, our children, and our grandchildren, would still be enslaved to Pharaoh in Egypt. [Therefore,] even if we were all wise, all men of understanding, all well-versed in Torah, we would still be commanded to tell about the Exodus from Egypt; and whoever discusses the Exodus from Egypt at length is praiseworthy.*

Ma-aseh b'rabi eli-ezer v'rabi y'hoshua
v'rabi el-özör ben azaryöh v'rabi
akivö v'rabi tarfon she-höyu m'subin
biv'nay v'rak. V'höyu m'sap'rim
bi-tzi-as mitzra-yim köl oso ha-lai'löh
ad she-bö-u salmi-dayhem v'öm'ru
löhem rabosaynu higi-a z'man
k'rias sh'ma shel shacharis.

מַעֲשֶׂה בְּרַבִּי אֱלִיעֶזֶר וְרַבִּי יְהוֹשֻׁעַ
וְרַבִּי אֶלְעָזָר בֶּן עֲזַרְיָה וְרַבִּי
עֲקִיבָא וְרַבִּי טַרְפוֹן שֶׁהָיוּ מְסֻבִּין
בִּבְנֵי בְרַק. וְהָיוּ מְסַפְּרִים
בִּיצִיאַת מִצְרַיִם כָּל אוֹתוֹ הַלַּיְלָה
עַד שֶׁבָּאוּ תַלְמִידֵיהֶם וְאָמְרוּ
לָהֶם רַבּוֹתֵינוּ הִגִּיעַ זְמַן
קְרִיאַת שְׁמַע שֶׁל שַׁחֲרִית:

*It happened that Rabbi Eliezer, Rabbi Yehoshua, Rabbi Elazar ben Azaryah, Rabbi Akiva, and Rabbi Tarphon were reclining [at the seder] in B'nei Berak. They discussed the Exodus from Egypt all that night, until their students came and told them: "Our teachers, the time for reciting the morning Shema has arrived."*

Ömar rabi el-özör ben azar-yöh haray
ani k'ven shiv-im shönö v'lo zöchisi
shetay-ömar y'tzi-as mitzra-yim
ba-laylos ad shed'röshöh ben zomöh.

אָמַר רַבִּי אֶלְעָזָר בֶּן עֲזַרְיָה הֲרֵי
אֲנִי כְּבֶן שִׁבְעִים שָׁנָה וְלֹא זָכִיתִי
שֶׁתֵּאָמֵר יְצִיאַת מִצְרַיִם
בַּלֵּילוֹת עַד שֶׁדְּרָשָׂהּ בֶּן זוֹמָא.

Shene-emar l'ma-an tizkor es yom
tzay-s'chö may-eretz mitzra-yim kol
y'may cha-yechö. Y'may cha-yechö
ha-yömim. Kol y'may cha-yechö
l'hövi ha-laylos. Va-cha-chömim
om'rim y'may cha-yechö hö-olöm
ha-zeh. Kol y'may cha-yechö l'hövi
limos ha-möshi-ach.

שֶׁנֶּאֱמַר לְמַעַן תִּזְכֹּר אֶת יוֹם
צֵאתְךָ מֵאֶרֶץ מִצְרַיִם כֹּל
יְמֵי חַיֶּיךָ. יְמֵי חַיֶּיךָ
הַיָּמִים. כֹּל יְמֵי חַיֶּיךָ
לְהָבִיא הַלֵּילוֹת. וַחֲכָמִים
אוֹמְרִים יְמֵי חַיֶּיךָ הָעוֹלָם
הַזֶּה. כֹּל יְמֵי חַיֶּיךָ לְהָבִיא
לִימוֹת הַמָּשִׁיחַ:

*Rabbi Elazar ben Azaryah said: I am like a seventy year-old man. Never-theless, I did not succeed in proving that the Exodus from Egypt must be mentioned at night until Ben Zoma explained it; as it is said: "So that you may remember the day you left Egypt all the days of your life." [The phrase] "the days of your life" refers to the days; [adding the word] "all" includes the nights as well. The Sages interpreted [the phrase] "the days of your life" as referring to the present-day world, and "all the days of your life" as including the Days of Moshiach.*

Böruch ha-mökom. Böruch hu.
Böruch shenösan toröh l'amo
yisrö-ayl. Böruch hu.
K'neged arbö-öh vönim dib'röh
soröh. Echöd chöchöm.
V'echöd röshö. V'echöd töm.
V'echöd she-ayno yoday-ah lish-ol.

בָּרוּךְ הַמָּקוֹם. בָּרוּךְ הוּא.
בָּרוּךְ שֶׁנָּתַן תּוֹרָה לְעַמּוֹ
יִשְׂרָאֵל. בָּרוּךְ הוּא.
כְּנֶגֶד אַרְבָּעָה בָנִים דִּבְּרָה
תּוֹרָה. אֶחָד חָכָם.
וְאֶחָד רָשָׁע. וְאֶחָד תָּם.
וְאֶחָד שֶׁאֵינוֹ יוֹדֵעַ לִשְׁאוֹל:

*Blessed is the Omnipresent, blessed be He. Blessed be He Who gave the Torah to*

*His people, Israel; blessed be He. The Torah speaks of four sons: one wise, and one wicked, and one simple, and one who does not know how to ask.*

Chöchöm mah hu omayr,    חָכָם מַה הוּא אוֹמֵר,

mö hö-aydos v'ha-chukim    מָה הָעֵדֹת וְהַחֻקִּים

v'ha-mishpötim asher tzivö adonöy    וְהַמִּשְׁפָּטִים אֲשֶׁר צִוָּה יְהֹוָה

elohay-chem es'chem v'af atöh emor    אֱלֹהֵינוּ אֶתְכֶם וְאַף אַתָּה אֱמֹר

lo k'hil'chos ha-pesach ayn maftirin    לוֹ כְּהִלְכוֹת הַפֶּסַח אֵין מַפְטִירִין

achar ha-pesach afikomön.    אַחַר הַפֶּסַח אֲפִיקוֹמָן:

*The wise son, what does he say? "What are the testimonies, statutes and laws that the Lord our God has commanded you?" You should reply to him, [teaching him] the laws of Pesach [until their conclusion]: One may not eat any dessert after the Pesach-offering.*

Röshö ma hu omayr, möh hö-avodöh    רָשָׁע מַה הוּא אוֹמֵר, מָה הָעֲבוֹדָה

ha-zos löchem. Löchem v'lo lo.    הַזֹּאת לָכֶם. לָכֶם וְלֹא לוֹ.

Ul'fi she-hotzi es atz-mo min ha-k'löl    וּלְפִי שֶׁהוֹצִיא אֶת עַצְמוֹ מִן הַכְּלָל

köfar b'ikör. V'af atöh hak-hay es    כָּפַר בְּעִקָּר. וְאַף אַתָּה הַקְהֵה אֶת

shinöv ve-emor lo, ba-avur zeh ösöh    שִׁנָּיו וֶאֱמֹר לוֹ, בַּעֲבוּר זֶה עָשָׂה

adonöy li b'tzaysi mimitzrö-yim.    יְהֹוָה לִי בְּצֵאתִי מִמִּצְרָיִם.

Li v'lo lo, ilu hö-yöh shöm    לִי וְלֹא לוֹ, אִלּוּ הָיָה שָׁם

lo hö-yöh nig-öl.    לֹא הָיָה נִגְאָל:

*The wicked son, what does he say? "What is this service to you?" [By saying] "to you," [he implies] "but not to himself." Since he excludes himself from our people at large, he denies the foundation of our faith. Therefore you should blunt his*

57

*teeth, and tell him: "It is because of this that the Lord did for me when I went out of Egypt," "for me" – but not for him! Had he been there, he would not have been redeemed.*

תָּם מַה הוּא אוֹמֵר, מַה זֹּאת.
וְאָמַרְתָּ אֵלָיו, בְּחֹזֶק יָד
הוֹצִיאָנוּ יְהֹוָה מִמִּצְרַיִם
מִבֵּית עֲבָדִים:

Töm mah hu omayr, mah zos.
V'ömartöh aylöv, b'chozek yöd
ho-tzi-önu adonöy mimitzra-yim
mibays avödim.

*The simple son, what does he say? "What is this?" You should tell him: "With a strong hand, the Lord brought us out from Egypt, from the house of bondage."*

וְשֶׁאֵינוֹ יוֹדֵעַ לִשְׁאוֹל אַתְּ פְּתַח
לוֹ, שֶׁנֶּאֱמַר, וְהִגַּדְתָּ לְבִנְךָ
בַּיּוֹם הַהוּא לֵאמֹר בַּעֲבוּר זֶה
עָשָׂה יְהֹוָה לִי בְּצֵאתִי מִמִּצְרָיִם:

V'she-ayno yoday-ah lish-ol at p'sach
lo, shene-emar, v'higad-tö l'vin'chö
ba-yom ha-hu laymor, ba-avur zeh
ösö adonöy li b'tzaysi mimitzrö-yim.

*The son who does not know how to ask, you must initiate him, as it is said: "You shall tell your son on that day: 'It is because of this that the Lord did for me when I went out of Egypt.' "*

יָכוֹל מֵרֹאשׁ חֹדֶשׁ תַּלְמוּד
לוֹמַר בַּיּוֹם הַהוּא, אִי בַּיּוֹם הַהוּא
יָכוֹל מִבְּעוֹד יוֹם תַּלְמוּד לוֹמַר
בַּעֲבוּר זֶה. בַּעֲבוּר זֶה לֹא אָמַרְתִּי
אֶלָּא בְּשָׁעָה שֶׁיֵּשׁ מַצָּה
וּמָרוֹר מֻנָּחִים לְפָנֶיךָ:

Yöchol mayrosh chodesh talmud
lomar ba-yom ha-hu, i ba-yom ha-hu
yöchol mib'od yom talmud lomar
ba-avur zeh. Ba-avur zeh lo ömarti
elö b'shö-öh she-yaysh matzöh
umöror mu-nöchim l'fönechö.

*One may think [that the obligation to discuss the Exodus begins] from the first day of the month [of Nissan]. The Torah therefore says, "[You shall tell your son] on that day," [i.e., on the day of the Exodus]. From the phrase "on that day," one might infer "while it is still day." [Hence,] the Torah adds "it is because of this." The expression 'because of this' implies that [the obligation only begins] when matzah and maror are placed before you.*

| | |
|---|---|
| Mit'chilöh ov'day avodöh zöröh höyu | מִתְּחִלָּה עוֹבְדֵי עֲבוֹדָה זָרָה הָיוּ |
| avosaynu v'ach-shöv kay-r'vönu | אֲבוֹתֵינוּ וְעַכְשָׁו קֵרְבָנוּ |
| ha-mökom la-avodöso. Shene-emar | הַמָּקוֹם לַעֲבוֹדָתוֹ. שֶׁנֶּאֱמַר |
| va-yomer y'hoshu-a el köl hö-öm | וַיֹּאמֶר יְהוֹשֻׁעַ אֶל כָּל הָעָם |
| ko ömar adonöy elohay yisrö-ayl | כֹּה אָמַר יְהֹוָה אֱלֹהֵי יִשְׂרָאֵל |
| b'ayver ha-nöhör yösh'vu avosaychem | בְּעֵבֶר הַנָּהָר יָשְׁבוּ אֲבוֹתֵיכֶם |
| may-olöm terach avi avröhöm va-avi | מֵעוֹלָם תֶּרַח אֲבִי אַבְרָהָם וַאֲבִי |
| nöchor va-ya-av'du elohim achay-rim. | נָחוֹר וַיַּעַבְדוּ אֱלֹהִים אֲחֵרִים: |

*In the beginning, our fathers worshipped idols, but now the Omnipresent has brought us close to His service, as it is said: "And Joshua said to all the people: So says the Lord, the God of Israel: 'Your fathers always dwelt beyond the [Euphrates] River – Terach, the father of Avraham and the father of Nachor, and they served other gods."*

| | |
|---|---|
| Vö-ekach es avichem es avröhöm | וָאֶקַּח אֶת אֲבִיכֶם אֶת אַבְרָהָם |
| may-ayver ha-nöhör vö-olaych oso | מֵעֵבֶר הַנָּהָר וָאוֹלֵךְ אוֹתוֹ |
| b'chöl eretz k'nö-an vö-arbeh es | בְּכָל אֶרֶץ כְּנַעַן וָאַרְבֶּה אֶת |
| za-ro vö-eten lo es yitzchök. | זַרְעוֹ וָאֶתֵּן לוֹ אֶת יִצְחָק: |
| Vö-etayn l'yitzchök es ya-akov v'es | וָאֶתֵּן לְיִצְחָק אֶת יַעֲקֹב וְאֶת |
| aysöv vö-etayn l'aysöv es har say-ir | עֵשָׂו וָאֶתֵּן לְעֵשָׂו אֶת הַר שֵׂעִיר |

lö-reshes oso v'ya-akov uvönöv
yör'du mitzrö-yim.

לָרֶשֶׁת אוֹתוֹ וְיַעֲקֹב וּבָנָיו
יָרְדוּ מִצְרָיִם :

*'And I took your father Avraham from beyond the river and led him throughout the land of Canaan. I multiplied his seed and I gave him Yitzchak. To Yitzchak I gave Yaakov and Esau. I gave Mount Seir to Esau as an inheritance, and Yaakov and his children went down to Egypt.'*

Böruch sho-mayr havtö-chöso
l'yisrö-ayl. Böruch hu. She-haködosh
böruch hu chi-shayv es ha-kaytz
la-asos k'mö she-ömar l'avröhöm
övinu biv'ris bayn ha-b'sörim.
Shene-emar va-yomer l'avröm
yödo-ah tayda ki gayr yih-yeh
zar-achö b'eretz lo löhem
va-avödum v'inu osöm arba
may-os shönöh. V'gam es ha-goy
asher ya-avodu dön önochi v'acharay
chayn yay-tz'u bir'chush gödol.

בָּרוּךְ שׁוֹמֵר הַבְטָחָתוֹ
לְיִשְׂרָאֵל. בָּרוּךְ הוּא. שֶׁהַקָּדוֹשׁ
בָּרוּךְ הוּא חִשֵּׁב אֶת הַקֵּץ
לַעֲשׂוֹת כְּמָה שֶׁאָמַר לְאַבְרָהָם
אָבִינוּ בִּבְרִית בֵּין הַבְּתָרִים.
שֶׁנֶּאֱמַר וַיֹּאמֶר לְאַבְרָם
יָדֹעַ תֵּדַע כִּי גֵר יִהְיֶה
זַרְעֲךָ בְּאֶרֶץ לֹא לָהֶם
וַעֲבָדוּם וְעִנּוּ אֹתָם אַרְבַּע
מֵאוֹת שָׁנָה : וְגַם אֶת הַגּוֹי
אֲשֶׁר יַעֲבֹדוּ דָּן אָנֹכִי וְאַחֲרֵי
כֵן יֵצְאוּ בִּרְכֻשׁ גָּדוֹל :

*Blessed is He Who keeps His promise to Israel, blessed be He. The Holy One, blessed be He, calculated the end [of the bondage] in order to do as He had said to Avraham our father at the 'Covenant between the Portions,' as it is said: "And He said to Avram: 'Know with certainty that your descendants will be strangers in a land which does not belong to them, and they will enslave them and oppress them for four hundred years. Ultimately, I will judge the nation which they shall serve, and afterwards they shall leave with great wealth.' "*

**Cover the matzah, lift up the cup of wine and recite the following:**

V'hi she-öm'döh la-avosaynu v'lönu · וְהִיא שֶׁעָמְדָה לַאֲבוֹתֵינוּ וְלָנוּ
shelo echöd bil'vad ömad ölaynu · שֶׁלֹּא אֶחָד בִּלְבַד עָמַד עָלֵינוּ
l'chalosaynu elö sheb'chöl dor vödor · לְכַלּוֹתֵנוּ אֶלָּא שֶׁבְּכָל דּוֹר וָדוֹר
om'dim ölaynu l'chalosaynu. · עוֹמְדִים עָלֵינוּ לְכַלּוֹתֵנוּ.
V'ha-ködosh böruch hu · וְהַקָּדוֹשׁ בָּרוּךְ הוּא
matzilaynu miyödöm. · מַצִּילֵנוּ מִיָּדָם׃

*And this is what has stood by our fathers and us, for not only one has risen up against us to annihilate us, but in every generation they rise up against us to annihilate us, and the Holy One, blessed be He, saves us from their hand.*

**Put down the cup of wine and uncover the matzah.**
**Continue below:**

Tzay ul'mad mah bi-kaysh lövön · צֵא וּלְמַד מַה בִּקֵּשׁ לָבָן
hö-arami la-asos l'ya-akov övinu. · הָאֲרַמִּי לַעֲשׂוֹת לְיַעֲקֹב אָבִינוּ.
She-par-oh lo gözar elö al ha-z'chörim · שֶׁפַּרְעֹה לֹא גָזַר אֶלָּא עַל הַזְּכָרִים
v'lövön bikaysh la-akor es ha-kol. · וְלָבָן בִּקֵּשׁ לַעֲקֹר אֶת הַכֹּל.
Shene-emar arami ovayd övi · שֶׁנֶּאֱמַר אֲרַמִּי אֹבֵד אָבִי
va-yayred mitzrai-y'möh va-yögör · וַיֵּרֶד מִצְרַיְמָה וַיָּגָר
shöm bim'say m'öt va-y'hi shöm · שָׁם בִּמְתֵי מְעָט וַיְהִי שָׁם
l'goy gödol ö-tzum vöröv. · לְגוֹי גָּדוֹל עָצוּם וָרָב׃

*Go out and learn what Lavan the Aramean wanted to do to our father, Yaakov. Pharaoh decreed only against the males, but Lavan wanted to uproot all, as it is said: "An Aramean sought to destroy my father, and he went down to Egypt and sojourned there with a small number of people, and he became a nation there, great, powerful, and numerous."*

Va-yayred mitz-rai-y'möh önus al pi ha-dibur. Va-yögör shöm m'lamayd shelo yörad ya-akov övinu l'hishta-kay-a b'mitzra-yim elö lögur shöm. Shene-emar va-yom'ru el par-oh lögur bö-öretz bönu ki ayn mir-eh latzon asher la-avödechö ki chövayd hörö-öv b'eretz k'nö-an v'atöh yaysh'vu nö avödechö b'eretz goshen.

וַיֵּרֶד מִצְרַיְמָה אָנוּס עַל פִּי הַדִּבּוּר. וַיָּגָר שָׁם מְלַמֵּד שֶׁלֹּא יָרַד יַעֲקֹב אָבִינוּ לְהִשְׁתַּקֵּעַ בְּמִצְרַיִם אֶלָּא לָגוּר שָׁם. שֶׁנֶּאֱמַר וַיֹּאמְרוּ אֶל פַּרְעֹה לָגוּר בָּאָרֶץ בָּאנוּ כִּי אֵין מִרְעֶה לַצֹּאן אֲשֶׁר לַעֲבָדֶיךָ כִּי כָבֵד הָרָעָב בְּאֶרֶץ כְּנַעַן וְעַתָּה יֵשְׁבוּ נָא עֲבָדֶיךָ בְּאֶרֶץ גֹּשֶׁן :

*"And he went down to Egypt" – compelled by Divine decree. "And sojourned there" – this teaches that our father Yaakov did not go down to Egypt with the intention of settling there, but merely to live there temporarily, as it is said: "And they (Yaakov's sons) told Pharaoh: 'We have come to sojourn in the land, for there is no pasture for the flocks of your servants, for the famine is severe in the land of Canaan, and now, please let your servants dwell in the land of Goshen.' "*

Bim'say m'öt k'möh shene-emar b'shiv-im nefesh yör'du avosechö mitz-röy-möh v'atöh sö-m'chö adonöy elo-hechö k'choch'vay ha-shöma-yim

בְּמְתֵי מְעָט כְּמָה שֶׁנֶּאֱמַר בְּשִׁבְעִים נֶפֶשׁ יָרְדוּ אֲבֹתֶיךָ מִצְרָיְמָה וְעַתָּה שָׂמְךָ יְהֹוָה אֱלֹהֶיךָ כְּכוֹכְבֵי הַשָּׁמַיִם

lörov. Va-y'hi shöm l'goy m'lamayd
she-höyu yisrö-ayl m'tzuyönim shöm.
Gödol ö-tzum k'mö shene-emar
uv'nay yisrö-ayl pöru va-yish-r'tzu
va-yirbu Va-ya-atz'mu bim'od m'od
va-timölay hö-öretz osöm.
Vöröv k'mö shene-emar vö-e-evor
öla-yich vö-er-aych misbo-seses
b'dömö-yich vö-omar löch
b'döma-yich cha-yii vö-omar
löch b'döma-yich cha-yi. R'vövö
k'tzemach ha-sö-deh n'satich va-tirbi
va-tig-d'li va-tövo-i ba-adi adö-yim
shöda-yim nöchonu us'öraych
tzimay-ach v'at ayrom v'er-yöh.

לָרֹב: וַיְהִי שָׁם לְגוֹי מְלַמֵּד
שֶׁהָיוּ יִשְׂרָאֵל מְצֻיָּנִים שָׁם:
גָּדוֹל עָצוּם כְּמָה שֶׁנֶּאֱמַר
וּבְנֵי יִשְׂרָאֵל פָּרוּ וַיִּשְׁרְצוּ
וַיִּרְבּוּ וַיַּעַצְמוּ בִּמְאֹד מְאֹד
וַתִּמָּלֵא הָאָרֶץ אֹתָם:
וָרָב כְּמָה שֶׁנֶּאֱמַר וָאֶעֱבֹר
עָלַיִךְ וָאֶרְאֵךְ מִתְבּוֹסֶסֶת
בְּדָמָיִךְ וָאֹמַר לָךְ
בְּדָמַיִךְ חֲיִי וָאֹמַר
לָךְ בְּדָמַיִךְ חֲיִי: רְבָבָה
כְּצֶמַח הַשָּׂדֶה נְתַתִּיךְ וַתִּרְבִּי
וַתִּגְדְּלִי וַתָּבֹאִי בַּעֲדִי עֲדָיִים
שָׁדַיִם נָכֹנוּ וּשְׂעָרֵךְ
צִמֵּחַ וְאַתְּ עֵרֹם וְעֶרְיָה:

*"With a small number of people" – as it is said: "With seventy individuals your fathers went down to Egypt, and now the Lord your God has made you as numerous as the stars of heaven." "And he became there a nation" – this teaches that [the Jews] were distinctive there. "Great, powerful" – as it is said: "And the Children of Israel were fruitful and increased abundantly and multiplied, and they became very, very powerful and the land became filled with them." "And numerous" – as it is said: "I passed over you and saw you wallowing in your blood and I said to you: 'Through your blood, you will live,' and I said to you: 'Through your blood, you will live.' I made you as numerous as the plants of the*

63

*field, and you increased and grew, and became very beautiful; [your] bosom developed and your hair grew, but you were uncovered and bare."*

| | |
|---|---|
| Va-yöray-u osönu ha-mitzrim va-y'anunu va-yit'nu ölaynu avodöh köshö. Va-yöray-u osönu ha-mitzrim k'mö shene-emar hövö nis-chak'möh lo pen yirbeh v'hö-yöh ki sikrenö milchömöh v'nosaf gam hu al son'aynu v'nilcham bönu v'ölö min hö-öretz. Va-y'anunu k'mö shene-emar va-yösimu ölöv söray misim l'ma-an anoso b'siv'losöm va-yiven öray mis-k'nos l'far-oh es pisom v'es ra-amsays. Vayit'nu ölaynu avodöh köshöh k'möh shene-emar va-ya-avidu mitzra-yim es b'nay yisrö-ayl b'förech. Va-y'mö-r'ru es cha-yayhem ba-avodöh köshö b'chomer uvil'vay-nim uv'chöl avodöh basö-deh ays köl avodösöm asher öv'du vöhem b'förech. | וַיָּרֵעוּ אֹתָנוּ הַמִּצְרִים וַיְעַנּוּנוּ וַיִּתְּנוּ עָלֵינוּ עֲבֹדָה קָשָׁה: וַיָּרֵעוּ אֹתָנוּ הַמִּצְרִים כְּמָה שֶׁנֶּאֱמַר הָבָה נִתְחַכְּמָה לוֹ פֶּן יִרְבֶּה וְהָיָה כִּי תִקְרֶאנָה מִלְחָמָה וְנוֹסַף גַּם הוּא עַל שֹׂנְאֵינוּ וְנִלְחַם בָּנוּ וְעָלָה מִן הָאָרֶץ: וַיְעַנּוּנוּ כְּמָה שֶׁנֶּאֱמַר וַיָּשִׂימוּ עָלָיו שָׂרֵי מִסִּים לְמַעַן עַנֹּתוֹ בְּסִבְלֹתָם וַיִּבֶן עָרֵי מִסְכְּנוֹת לְפַרְעֹה אֶת פִּתֹם וְאֶת רַעַמְסֵס: וַיִּתְּנוּ עָלֵינוּ עֲבֹדָה קָשָׁה כְּמָה שֶׁנֶּאֱמַר וַיַּעֲבִדוּ מִצְרַיִם אֶת בְּנֵי יִשְׂרָאֵל בְּפָרֶךְ: וַיְמָרְרוּ אֶת חַיֵּיהֶם בַּעֲבֹדָה קָשָׁה בְּחֹמֶר וּבִלְבֵנִים וּבְכָל עֲבֹדָה בַּשָּׂדֶה אֵת כָּל עֲבֹדָתָם אֲשֶׁר עָבְדוּ בָהֶם בְּפָרֶךְ: |

*"And the Egyptians treated us badly and they made us suffer, and they imposed harsh labor upon us." "And the Egyptians treated us badly" – as it is said: "Come, let us act cunningly with them lest they multiply, and then, if there should be a*

*war, they may join our enemies, and wage war against us and leave the land."
"And they made us suffer" – as it is said: "They placed taskmasters over them in
order to oppress them with their burdens, and they built storage cities for
Pharaoh, Pitom and Raamseis." "And they imposed harsh labor upon us" – as it
is said: "And the Egyptians made the Children of Israel to serve with rigor. They
embittered their lives with harsh labor, with mortar and bricks, as well as with all
kinds of labor of the field; all their toil which they made them serve was with
rigor."*

| | |
|---:|:---|
| Vanitz-ak el adonöy elohay avosaynu | וַנִּצְעַק אֶל יְהֹוָה אֱלֹהֵי אֲבוֹתֵינוּ |
| va-yishma adonöy es ko-laynu | וַיִּשְׁמַע יְהֹוָה אֶת קֹלֵנוּ |
| va-yar es ön-yaynu v'es amölaynu v'es | וַיַּרְא אֶת עָנְיֵנוּ וְאֶת עֲמָלֵנוּ וְאֶת |
| la-chatzaynu. Vanitz-ak el adonöy | לַחֲצֵנוּ : וַנִּצְעַק אֶל יְהֹוָה |
| elohay avosaynu k'möh shene-emar | אֱלֹהֵי אֲבוֹתֵינוּ כְּמָה שֶׁנֶּאֱמַר |
| va-y'hi va-yömim hö-rabim hö-haym | וַיְהִי בַיָּמִים הָרַבִּים הָהֵם |
| va-yömös melech mitzra-yim | וַיָּמָת מֶלֶךְ מִצְרַיִם |
| va-yay-ön'chu v'nay yisrö-ayl | וַיֵּאָנְחוּ בְנֵי יִשְׂרָאֵל |
| min hö-avodöh va-yiz-öku va-ta-al | מִן הָעֲבֹדָה וַיִּזְעָקוּ וַתַּעַל |
| shav-ösöm el hö-elohim | שַׁוְעָתָם אֶל הָאֱלֹהִים |
| min hö-avodöh. | מִן הָעֲבֹדָה : |

*"And we cried out to the Lord the God of our fathers, and the Lord heard our
voice, He saw our suffering, our difficult labor, and our oppression." "And we
cried out to the Lord the God of our fathers –as it is said: "And it came to pass
after those many days, that the king of Egypt died, and the Children of Israel
groaned from the work, and they cried out, and their outcry went up to God from
the work."*

Va-yishma adonöy es kolaynu k'möh
shene-emar va-yishma elohim es
na-akösöm va-yizkor elohim es briso
es avröhöm es yitzchök v'es ya-akov.

וַיִּשְׁמַע יְהֹוָה אֶת קֹלֵנוּ כְּמָה
שֶׁנֶּאֱמַר וַיִּשְׁמַע אֱלֹהִים אֶת
נַאֲקָתָם וַיִּזְכֹּר אֱלֹהִים אֶת בְּרִיתוֹ
אֶת אַבְרָהָם אֶת יִצְחָק וְאֶת יַעֲקֹב:

*"And the Lord heard our voice" – as it is said: "And God heard their cries, and God remembered His covenant with Avraham, Yitzchak, and Yaakov."*

Va-yar es ön'yaynu zo p'rishus derech
eretz k'möh shene-emar va-yar elohim
es b'nay yisrö-ayl va-yayda elohim.

וַיַּרְא אֶת עָנְיֵנוּ זוֹ פְּרִישׁוּת דֶּרֶךְ
אֶרֶץ כְּמָה שֶׁנֶּאֱמַר וַיַּרְא אֱלֹהִים
אֶת בְּנֵי יִשְׂרָאֵל וַיֵּדַע אֱלֹהִים:

*"And He saw our suffering" – this refers to the disruption of family life, as it is said: "And God saw the Children of Israel and God took note."*

V'es amölaynu aylu ha-bönim k'möh
shene-emar köl ha-bayn ha-yilod
ha-y'oröh tashli-chuhu v'chöl ha-bas
t'cha-yun. V'es la-chatzaynu zeh
ha-d'chak kmöh shene-emar v'gam
rö-isi es ha-lachatz asher mitzra-yim
lochatzim osöm.

וְאֶת עֲמָלֵנוּ אֵלּוּ הַבָּנִים כְּמָה
שֶׁנֶּאֱמַר כָּל הַבֵּן הַיִּלוֹד
הַיְאֹרָה תַּשְׁלִיכֻהוּ וְכָל הַבַּת
תְּחַיּוּן: וְאֶת לַחֲצֵנוּ זֶה
הַדְּחַק כְּמָה שֶׁנֶּאֱמַר וְגַם
רָאִיתִי אֶת הַלַּחַץ אֲשֶׁר מִצְרַיִם
לוֹחֲצִים אֹתָם:

*"And our difficult labor" – this refers to the children, as it is said: "Every boy that is born you shall throw into the river, and every girl you shall keep alive." "And our oppression" – this refers to the pressure, as it is said: "I have also seen the oppression with which the Egyptians oppress them."*

Va-yo-tzi-aynu adonöy mimitzra-yim
b'yöd chazököh uviz'ro-a n'tu-yöh
uv'morö gödol uv'osos uv'mof'sim.
Va-yo-tzi-aynu adonöy mimitzra-yim
lo al y'day mal-öch v'lo al y'day
söröf v'lo al y'day shöli-ach elö
ha-ködosh böruch hu bich'vodo
uv'atzmo. Shene-emar v'övarti
v'eretz mitzra-yim ba-lai-y'löh ha-zeh
v'hikaysi chöl b'chor b'eretz
mitzra-yim may-ödöm v'ad b'haymöh
uv'chöl elohay mitzra-yim e-eseh
sh'fötim ani adonöy. V'övar'ti v'eretz
mitzra-yim ani v'lo mal-öch. V'hikaysi
chöl b'chor b'eretz mitzra-yim ani
v'lo söröf. Uv'chöl elohay mitzra-yim
e-eseh sh'fötim ani v'lo ha-shöli-ach.
Ani adonöy, ani hu v'lo achayr.

וַיּוֹצִיאֵנוּ יְהוָֹה מִמִּצְרַיִם
בְּיָד חֲזָקָה וּבִזְרוֹעַ נְטוּיָה
וּבְמֹרָא גָדוֹל וּבְאֹתוֹת וּבְמֹפְתִים:
וַיּוֹצִיאֵנוּ יְהוָֹה מִמִּצְרַיִם
לֹא עַל יְדֵי מַלְאָךְ וְלֹא עַל יְדֵי
שָׂרָף וְלֹא עַל יְדֵי שָׁלִיחַ אֶלָּא
הַקָּדוֹשׁ בָּרוּךְ הוּא בִּכְבוֹדוֹ
וּבְעַצְמוֹ. שֶׁנֶּאֱמַר וְעָבַרְתִּי
בְאֶרֶץ מִצְרַיִם בַּלַּיְלָה הַזֶּה
וְהִכֵּיתִי כָל בְּכוֹר בְּאֶרֶץ
מִצְרַיִם מֵאָדָם וְעַד בְּהֵמָה
וּבְכָל אֱלֹהֵי מִצְרַיִם אֶעֱשֶׂה
שְׁפָטִים אֲנִי יְהוָֹה: וְעָבַרְתִּי בְאֶרֶץ
מִצְרַיִם אֲנִי וְלֹא מַלְאָךְ. וְהִכֵּיתִי
כָל בְּכוֹר בְּאֶרֶץ מִצְרַיִם אֲנִי
וְלֹא שָׂרָף. וּבְכָל אֱלֹהֵי מִצְרַיִם
אֶעֱשֶׂה שְׁפָטִים אֲנִי וְלֹא הַשָּׁלִיחַ.
אֲנִי יְהוָֹה, אֲנִי הוּא וְלֹא אַחֵר:

*"And the Lord brought us out of Egypt with a strong hand, with an outstretched arm, with great manifestations, and with signs and wonders." "And the Lord brought us out of Egypt" – not through an angel, not through a seraph, not through a messenger, but the Holy One, blessed be He, in His glory and by Himself, as it is said: "And I will pass through the land of Egypt on that night and I will slay every firstborn in the land of Egypt, from man to beast, and against all*

*the gods of Egypt I shall execute judgments, I am the Lord." "And I will pass through the land of Egypt" – I and not an angel; "And I will slay every firstborn" – I and not a seraph; "And against all the gods of Egypt I shall execute judgments" – I and not the messenger; "I am the Lord" – it is I and no other.*

B'yöd chazököh zeh ha-dever k'möh shene-emar hinay yad adonöy ho-yöh b'mik-n'chö asher basö-deh basusim ba-chamorim ba-g'malim ba-bökör uva-tzon dever kövayd m'od. Uviz'ro-a n'tu-yö zo ha-cherev k'möh shene-emar v'char'bo sh'luföh b'yödo n'tu-yöh al y'rushölö-yim. Uv'morö gödol zeh giluy sh'chinöh k'möh shene-emar o ha-nisöh elohim lövo lökachas lo goy mi-kerev goy b'masos b'osos uv'mof'sim uv'mil-chömöh uv'yöd chazököh uviz'ro-a n'tu-yö uv'morö-im g'dolim k'chol asher ösö lö-chem adonöy elohay-chem b'mitzra-yim l'aynechö. Uv'osos zeh ha-mateh k'möh shene-emar v'es ha-mateh ha-zeh tikach b'yödechö asher ta-aseh bo es hö-osos.

בְּיָד חֲזָקָה זֶה הַדֶּבֶר כְּמָה
שֶׁנֶּאֱמַר הִנֵּה יַד יְהֹוָה הוֹיָה
בְּמִקְנְךָ אֲשֶׁר בַּשָּׂדֶה בַּסּוּסִים
בַּחֲמֹרִים בַּגְּמַלִּים בַּבָּקָר
וּבַצֹּאן דֶּבֶר כָּבֵד מְאֹד:
וּבִזְרֹעַ נְטוּיָה זוֹ הַחֶרֶב כְּמָה
שֶׁנֶּאֱמַר וְחַרְבּוֹ שְׁלוּפָה בְּיָדוֹ
נְטוּיָה עַל יְרוּשָׁלָיִם. וּבְמֹרָא
גָדֹל זֶה גִּלּוּי שְׁכִינָה כְּמָה
שֶׁנֶּאֱמַר אוֹ הֲנִסָּה אֱלֹהִים לָבֹא
לָקַחַת לוֹ גוֹי מִקֶּרֶב גּוֹי בְּמַסֹּת
בְּאֹתֹת וּבְמוֹפְתִים וּבְמִלְחָמָה
וּבְיָד חֲזָקָה וּבִזְרֹעַ נְטוּיָה
וּבְמוֹרָאִים גְּדֹלִים כְּכֹל אֲשֶׁר
עָשָׂה לָכֶם יְהֹוָה אֱלֹהֵיכֶם
בְּמִצְרַיִם לְעֵינֶיךָ: וּבְאֹתוֹת זֶה
הַמַּטֶּה כְּמָה שֶׁנֶּאֱמַר וְאֶת
הַמַּטֶּה הַזֶּה תִּקַּח בְּיָדֶךָ
אֲשֶׁר תַּעֲשֶׂה בּוֹ אֶת הָאֹתֹת:

Uv'mof'sim zeh ha-döm k'möh    וּבְמוֹפְתִים זֶה הַדָּם כְּמָה
shene-emar v'nösati mof'sim    שֶׁנֶּאֱמַר וְנָתַתִּי מִפְתִים
ba-shöma-yim uvö-öretz.    : בַּשָּׁמַיִם וּבָאָרֶץ

*"With a strong hand" – this refers to the pestilence, as it is said: "Behold, the hand of the Lord will be on your livestock that are in the field, on the horses, on the donkeys, on the camels, on the herds and on the flocks, a very severe pestilence." "And with an outstretched arm" – this refers to the sword, as it is said: "His sword was drawn in his hand, stretched out over Jerusalem." "And with great manifestations" – this refers to the revelation of the Divine Presence, as it is said: "Has any god ever miraculously come to take for himself a nation from amidst a nation with trials, with signs, and with wonders, and with war, and with a strong hand and with an outstretched arm, and with great manifestations, like all that the Lord your God did for you in Egypt before your eyes?" "And with signs" – this refers to the staff, as it is said: "Take this staff in your hand, with which you shall perform the signs." "And with wonders" – this refers to the blood, as it is said: "And I will show wonders in heaven and on earth...*

**When saying the following passage spill three drops of wine from your cup into a dish or bowl:**

Döm, vö-aysh, v'sim'ros öshön.    : דָּם, וָאֵשׁ, וְתִימְרוֹת עָשָׁן

*...blood, and fire, and pillars of smoke."*

Dövör achayr b'yöd chazököh    דָּבָר אַחֵר בְּיָד חֲזָקָה
shta-yim. Uviz'ro-a n'tu-yö shta-yim.    שְׁתַּיִם. וּבִזְרוֹעַ נְטוּיָה שְׁתַּיִם.
Uv'morö gödol shta-yim. Uv'osos    וּבְמוֹרָא גָּדוֹל שְׁתַּיִם. וּבְאֹתוֹת
shta-yim. Uv'mof'sim shta-yim.    : שְׁתַּיִם. וּבְמֹפְתִים שְׁתַּיִם

*Another explanation [associating each phrase with two plagues]: "With a strong hand": two; "and with an outstretched arm": two; "and with great manifestations": two; "and with signs": two; "and with wonders": two.*

Aylu eser makos she-hayvi ha-ködosh אֵלּוּ עֶשֶׂר מַכּוֹת שֶׁהֵבִיא הַקָּדוֹשׁ
böruch hu al ha-mitzrim b'mitzra-yim. בָּרוּךְ הוּא עַל הַמִּצְרִים בְּמִצְרַיִם.
V'aylu hayn: וְאֵלּוּ הֵן:

*These are the ten plagues which the Holy One, blessed be He, brought upon the Egyptians in Egypt: They are:*

**When saying each of the ten plagues spill some wine from your cup into a dish or bowl:**

Döm. Tz'farday-a. Kinim. Örov. דָּם. צְפַרְדֵּעַ. כִּנִּים. עָרוֹב.
Dever. Sh'chin. Böröd. Arbeh. דֶּבֶר. שְׁחִין. בָּרָד. אַרְבֶּה.
Choshech. Makas B'choros. חֹשֶׁךְ. מַכַּת בְּכוֹרוֹת:

*Blood, Frogs, Lice, Wild Beasts, Pestilence, Boils, Hail, Locusts, Darkness, Slaying of the Firstborn.*

**When saying each of the following three acronyms (of the ten plagues) spill some wine from your cup into a dish or bowl:**

Rabi y'hudöh hö-yöh nosayn böhem רַבִּי יְהוּדָה הָיָה נוֹתֵן בָּהֶם
simönim: D'tzach. Adash. B'achav. סִמָּנִים: דְּצַ"ךְ. עֲדַ"שׁ. בְּאַחַ"ב:

*Rabbi Yehudah referred to them by the acronyms: detzach, adash, be'achav.*

**The spilled wine is collected from all in a large bowl and removed from the table and discarded. Top off your cup with wine and continue below.**

Rabi yosay ha-g'lili omayr mina-yin
atöh omayr she-löku ha-mitzrim
b'mitzra-yim eser makos v'al
ha-yöm löku cha-mishim makos.
B'mitzra-yim mah hu omayr
va-yom'ru ha-char'tumim el par-oh
etzba elohim hi. V'al ha-yöm mah
hu omayr va-yar yisrö-ayl es ha-yöd
ha-g'dolöh asher ösö adonöy
b'mitzra-yim va-yi-r'u hö-öm es adonöy
va-ya-aminu ba-donöy uv'mosheh
avdo. Kamöh löku v'etzba eser
makos. Emor may-atöh b'mitzra-yim
löku eser makos, v'al ha-yöm
löku chamishim makos.

רַבִּי יוֹסֵי הַגְּלִילִי אוֹמֵר מִנַּיִן
אַתָּה אוֹמֵר שֶׁלָּקוּ הַמִּצְרִים
בְּמִצְרַיִם עֶשֶׂר מַכּוֹת וְעַל
הַיָּם לָקוּ חֲמִשִּׁים מַכּוֹת.
בְּמִצְרַיִם מַה הוּא אוֹמֵר
וַיֹּאמְרוּ הַחַרְטֻמִּים אֶל פַּרְעֹה
אֶצְבַּע אֱלֹהִים הִיא. וְעַל הַיָּם מַה
הוּא אוֹמֵר וַיַּרְא יִשְׂרָאֵל אֶת הַיָּד
הַגְּדוֹלָה אֲשֶׁר עָשָׂה יְהֹוָה
בְּמִצְרַיִם וַיִּירְאוּ הָעָם אֶת יְהֹוָה
וַיַּאֲמִינוּ בַּיהֹוָה וּבְמֹשֶׁה
עַבְדּוֹ: כַּמָּה לָקוּ בְאֶצְבַּע עֶשֶׂר
מַכּוֹת. אֱמֹר מֵעַתָּה בְּמִצְרַיִם
לָקוּ עֶשֶׂר מַכּוֹת, וְעַל הַיָּם
לָקוּ חֲמִשִּׁים מַכּוֹת:

*Rabbi Yossi the Gallilean said: How do you know that the Egyptians were struck by ten plagues in Egypt and were struck by fifty plagues at the Sea? Concerning [the plagues in] Egypt, it says: "The magicians said to Pharaoh: 'This is the finger of God.' " And [concerning the plagues] at the sea, it says: "And Israel saw the great hand which the Lord wielded against Egypt, the people feared the Lord, and they believed in the Lord and in Moshe His servant." With how many plagues were they struck by "the finger"? Ten. Thus, we may conclude that in Egypt they were struck by ten plagues and at the sea they were struck by fifty plagues.*

Rabi eli-ezer omayr mina-yin she-köl maköh umaköh she-hayvi ha-ködosh böruch hu al ha-mitz-rim b'mitzra-yim hö-y'söh shel arba makos. Shene-emar y'shalach böm charon apo evrö vö-za-am v'tzöröh mishla-chas mal-achay rö-im. Evröh achas. Vö-za-am shta-yim. V'tzöröh shölosh. Mishla-chas mal-achay rö-im arba. Emor may-atöh b'mitzra-yim löku arbö-im makos. V'al ha-yöm löku mösa-yim makos.

רַבִּי אֱלִיעֶזֶר אוֹמֵר מִנַּיִן שֶׁכָּל מַכָּה וּמַכָּה שֶׁהֵבִיא הַקָּדוֹשׁ בָּרוּךְ הוּא עַל הַמִּצְרִים בְּמִצְרַיִם הָיְתָה שֶׁל אַרְבַּע מַכּוֹת. שֶׁנֶּאֱמַר יְשַׁלַּח בָּם חֲרוֹן אַפּוֹ עֶבְרָה וָזַעַם וְצָרָה מִשְׁלַחַת מַלְאֲכֵי רָעִים: עֶבְרָה אַחַת. וָזַעַם שְׁתַּיִם. וְצָרָה שָׁלֹשׁ. מִשְׁלַחַת מַלְאֲכֵי רָעִים אַרְבַּע. אֱמֹר מֵעַתָּה בְּמִצְרַיִם לָקוּ אַרְבָּעִים מַכּוֹת. וְעַל הַיָּם לָקוּ מָאתַיִם מַכּוֹת:

*Rabbi Eliezer said: Which source teaches that every plague that the Holy One, blessed be He, brought upon the Egyptians in Egypt consisted of four plagues? For it is said: "He sent upon them His fierce anger: wrath, fury, trouble, and a band of emissaries of evil." "Wrath" [refers to] one plague; "fury" to a second; "trouble" to a third; and "a band of emissaries of evil" to a fourth. Thus, we may conclude that in Egypt they were struck by forty plagues and at the sea by two hundred plagues.*

רַבִּי עֲקִיבָא אוֹמֵר מִנַּיִן שֶׁכָּל
מַכָּה וּמַכָּה שֶׁהֵבִיא הַקָּדוֹשׁ
בָּרוּךְ הוּא עַל הַמִּצְרִים
בְּמִצְרַיִם הָיְתָה שֶׁל חָמֵשׁ
מַכּוֹת. שֶׁנֶּאֱמַר יְשַׁלַּח בָּם
חֲרוֹן אַפּוֹ עֶבְרָה וָזַעַם וְצָרָה
מִשְׁלַחַת מַלְאֲכֵי רָעִים. חֲרוֹן
אַפּוֹ אַחַת. עֶבְרָה שְׁתַּיִם. וָזַעַם
שָׁלֹשׁ. וְצָרָה אַרְבַּע. מִשְׁלַחַת
מַלְאֲכֵי רָעִים חָמֵשׁ. אֱמֹר
מֵעַתָּה בְּמִצְרַיִם לָקוּ
חֲמִשִּׁים מַכּוֹת. וְעַל הַיָּם
לָקוּ חֲמִשִּׁים וּמָאתַיִם מַכּוֹת׃

Rabi akivöh omayr mina-yin she-köl maköh umaköh she-hayvi ha-ködosh böruch hu al ha-mitz-rim b'mitzra-yim hö-y'söh shel chö-maysh makos. Shene-emar y'shalach böm charon apo evrö vö-za-am v'tzöröh mishla-chas mal'achay rö-im. Charon apo achas. Evröh shta-yim. Vö-za-am shölosh. V'tzöro arba. Mishla-chas mal-achay rö-im chömaysh. Emor may-atöh b'mitzra-yim löku chamishim makos. V'al ha-yöm löku chamishim umösa-yim makos

*Rabbi Akiva said: Which source teaches that every plague that the Holy One, blessed be He, brought upon the Egyptians consisted of five plagues? For it is said: "He sent upon them His fierce anger, wrath, fury, trouble, and a band of emissaries of evil." "His fierce anger" [refers to] one plague; "wrath" to a second; "fury" to a third; "trouble" to a fourth; and "a band of emissaries of evil" to a fifth. Thus, we may conclude that in Egypt they were struck by fifty plagues and at the sea by two hundred and fifty plagues.*

כַּמָּה מַעֲלוֹת טוֹבוֹת
לַמָּקוֹם עָלֵינוּ׃

Kamö ma-alos tovos la-mökom ölaynu.

*How many levels of favors has the Omnipresent bestowed upon us:*

| | |
|---|---|
| Ilu ho-tzi-önu mimitzra-yim v'lo ösöh | אִלּוּ הוֹצִיאָנוּ מִמִּצְרַיִם וְלֹא עָשָׂה |
| vö-hem sh'fötim da-yaynu. | בָּהֶם שְׁפָטִים דַּיֵּנוּ: |
| Ilu ösöh vöhem sh'fötim v'lo ösö | אִלּוּ עָשָׂה בָּהֶם שְׁפָטִים וְלֹא עָשָׂה |
| vaylo-hay-hem da-yaynu. | בֵאלֹהֵיהֶם דַּיֵּנוּ: |
| Ilu ösö vay-lohay-hem v'lo hörag | אִלּוּ עָשָׂה בֵאלֹהֵיהֶם וְלֹא הָרַג |
| es b'cho-rayhem da-yaynu. | אֶת בְּכוֹרֵיהֶם דַּיֵּנוּ: |
| Ilu hörag es b'cho-rayhem v'lo nösan | אִלּוּ הָרַג אֶת בְּכוֹרֵיהֶם וְלֹא נָתַן |
| lönu es mömonöm da-yaynu. | לָנוּ אֶת מָמוֹנָם דַּיֵּנוּ: |
| Ilu nösan lönu es mömonöm v'lo | אִלּוּ נָתַן לָנוּ אֶת מָמוֹנָם וְלֹא |
| köra lönu es ha-yöm da-yaynu. | קָרַע לָנוּ אֶת הַיָּם דַּיֵּנוּ: |
| Ilu köra lönu es ha-yöm | אִלּוּ קָרַע לָנוּ אֶת הַיָּם |
| v'lo he-evirönu v'socho | וְלֹא הֶעֱבִירָנוּ בְּתוֹכוֹ |
| bechö-rövöh da-yaynu. | בֶּחָרָבָה דַּיֵּנוּ: |
| Ilu he-evirönu v'socho | אִלּוּ הֶעֱבִירָנוּ בְּתוֹכוֹ |
| bechö-rövöh v'lo shika | בֶּחָרָבָה וְלֹא שָׁקַע |
| tzöraynu b'socho da-yaynu. | צָרֵינוּ בְּתוֹכוֹ דַּיֵּנוּ: |
| Ilu shika tzöraynu b'socho | אִלּוּ שָׁקַע צָרֵינוּ בְּתוֹכוֹ |
| v'lo sipayk tzörkaynu ba-midbör | וְלֹא סִפֵּק צָרְכֵּנוּ בַּמִּדְבָּר |
| arböim shönö da-yaynu. | אַרְבָּעִים שָׁנָה דַּיֵּנוּ: |
| Ilu sipayk tzörkaynu ba-midbör | אִלּוּ סִפֵּק צָרְכֵּנוּ בַּמִּדְבָּר |
| arböim shönö v'lo he-echilönu | אַרְבָּעִים שָׁנָה וְלֹא הֶאֱכִילָנוּ |
| es ha-mön da-yaynu. | אֶת הַמָּן דַּיֵּנוּ: |
| Ilu he-echilönu es ha-mön v'lo nösan | אִלּוּ הֶאֱכִילָנוּ אֶת הַמָּן וְלֹא נָתַן |
| lönu es ha-shabös da-yaynu. | לָנוּ אֶת הַשַּׁבָּת דַּיֵּנוּ: |

Ilu nösan lönu es ha-shabös v'lo אִלּוּ נָתַן לָנוּ אֶת הַשַּׁבָּת וְלֹא
kay-r'vönu lif'nay har sinai da-yaynu. קֵרְבָנוּ לִפְנֵי הַר סִינַי דַּיֵּנוּ:
Ilu kayr'vönu lif'nay har sinai v'lo אִלּוּ קֵרְבָנוּ לִפְנֵי הַר סִינַי וְלֹא
nösan lönu es ha-toröh da-yaynu. נָתַן לָנוּ אֶת הַתּוֹרָה דַּיֵּנוּ:
Ilu nösan lönu es ha-toröh v'lo אִלּוּ נָתַן לָנוּ אֶת הַתּוֹרָה וְלֹא
hich-nisönu l'eretz yisrö-ayl da-yaynu. הִכְנִיסָנוּ לְאֶרֶץ יִשְׂרָאֵל דַּיֵּנוּ:
Ilu hich-nisönu l'eretz yisrö-ayl אִלּוּ הִכְנִיסָנוּ לְאֶרֶץ יִשְׂרָאֵל
v'lo vönö lönu es bays וְלֹא בָנָה לָנוּ אֶת בֵּית
ha-b'chiröh da-yaynu. הַבְּחִירָה דַּיֵּנוּ:

*If He had brought us out of Egypt, and not executed judgments upon the Egyptians, it would have sufficed us! If He had executed judgments against them, and not against their gods, it would have sufficed us! If He had executed judgments against their gods, and not slain their firstborn, it would have sufficed us! If He had slain their firstborn, and not given us their wealth, it would have sufficed us! If He had given us their wealth, and not split the sea for us, it would have sufficed us! If He had split the sea for us, and not led us through it on dry land, it would have sufficed us! If He had led us through it on dry land, and not drowned our oppressors in it, it would have sufficed us! If He had drowned our oppressors in it, and not provided for our needs in the wilderness for forty years, it would have sufficed us! If He had provided for our needs in the wilderness for forty years, and not sustained us with the manna, it would have sufficed us! If He had sustained us with the manna, and not given us the Shabbat, it would have sufficed us! If He had given us the Shabbat, and not brought us before Mount Sinai, it would have sufficed us! If He had brought us before Mount Sinai, and not given us the Torah, it would have sufficed us! If He had given us the Torah, and not brought us into Eretz Yisrael, it would have sufficed us! If He had brought us into*

*Eretz Yisrael, and not built for us the Beit Habechirah [the chosen house, i.e. the Beit Hamikdash] it would have sufficed us!*

| | |
|---|---|
| Al achas kamöh v'chamöh | עַל אַחַת כַּמָּה וְכַמָּה |
| tovöh ch'fulöh um'chupeles | טוֹבָה כְפוּלָה וּמְכֻפֶּלֶת |
| la-mökom ölaynu. She-ho-tzi-önu | לַמָּקוֹם עָלֵינוּ. שֶׁהוֹצִיאָנוּ |
| mimitzrö-yim. V'ösö vöhem sh'fötim. | מִמִּצְרַיִם. וְעָשָׂה בָהֶם שְׁפָטִים. |
| V'ösöh vay-lohay-hem. V'hörag es | וְעָשָׂה בֵאלֹהֵיהֶם. וְהָרַג אֶת |
| b'cho-rayhem. V'nösan lönu es | בְּכוֹרֵיהֶם. וְנָתַן לָנוּ אֶת |
| mömonöm. V'köra lönu es ha-yöm. | מָמוֹנָם. וְקָרַע לָנוּ אֶת הַיָּם. |
| V'he-evirönu v'socho bechö-rövöh. | וְהֶעֱבִירָנוּ בְתוֹכוֹ בֶּחָרָבָה. |
| V'shika tzöraynu b'socho. V'sipayk | וְשִׁקַּע צָרֵינוּ בְּתוֹכוֹ. וְסִפֵּק |
| tzörkaynu ba-midbör arböim shönö. | צָרְכֵּנוּ בַּמִּדְבָּר אַרְבָּעִים שָׁנָה. |
| V'he-echilönu es ha-mön. V'nösan | וְהֶאֱכִילָנוּ אֶת הַמָּן. וְנָתַן |
| lönu es ha-shabös. V'kay-r'vönu lif'nay | לָנוּ אֶת הַשַּׁבָּת. וְקֵרְבָנוּ לִפְנֵי |
| har sinai. V'nösan lönu es ha-toröh. | הַר סִינַי. וְנָתַן לָנוּ אֶת הַתּוֹרָה. |
| V'hich-nisönu l'eretz yisrö-ayl. | וְהִכְנִיסָנוּ לְאֶרֶץ יִשְׂרָאֵל. |
| Uvönö lönu es bays ha-b'chiröh | וּבָנָה לָנוּ אֶת בֵּית הַבְּחִירָה |
| l'chapayr al köl avono-saynu. | לְכַפֵּר עַל כָּל עֲוֹנוֹתֵינוּ: |

*Thus, how much more so [do we owe thanks] to the Omnipresent for the repeated and manifold favors He bestowed upon us: He brought us out of Egypt; He executed judgments against the Egyptians; He executed judgments against their gods; He slew their firstborn; He gave us their wealth; He split the sea for us; He led us through it on dry land; He drowned our oppressors in it; He provided for our needs in the wilderness for forty years; He sustained us with the manna; He* gave us the Shabbat; He brought us before Mount Sinai; He gave us the Torah; He brought us into Eretz Yisrael; He built for us the Beit Habechirah to atone for all our sins.

Rabön gamli-ayl hö-yöh omayr, köl shelo ömar sh'loshöh d'vörim aylu ba-pesach lo yö-tzöh y'day chovöso. V'aylu hayn: Pesach, matzöh, umöror.

רַבָּן גַּמְלִיאֵל הָיָה אוֹמֵר, כָּל שֶׁלֹּא אָמַר שְׁלֹשָׁה דְבָרִים אֵלּוּ בַּפֶּסַח לֹא יָצָא יְדֵי חוֹבָתוֹ. וְאֵלּוּ הֵן: פֶּסַח, מַצָּה, וּמָרוֹר:

*Rabban Gamliel would say: "Whoever has not explained the following three things on Pesach [at the seder] has not fulfilled his obligation: They are Pesach (the Pesach-offering), matzah (the unleavened bread), and maror (the bitter herbs)."*

Pesach she-höyu avo-saynu och'lim biz'man she-bays ha-mikdösh ka-yöm, al shum möh. Al shum she-pösach ha-mökom al bötay avo-saynu b'mitzrö-yim. Shene-emar va-amar-tem zevach pesach hu la-donöy asher pösach al bötay v'nay yisrö-ayl b'mitzra-yim b'nögpo es mitzra-yim v'es bötaynu hitzil va-yikod hö-öm va-yish-tachavu.

פֶּסַח שֶׁהָיוּ אֲבוֹתֵינוּ אוֹכְלִים בִּזְמַן שֶׁבֵּית הַמִּקְדָּשׁ קַיָּם, עַל שׁוּם מָה. עַל שׁוּם שֶׁפָּסַח הַמָּקוֹם עַל בָּתֵּי אֲבוֹתֵינוּ בְּמִצְרָיִם. שֶׁנֶּאֱמַר וַאֲמַרְתֶּם זֶבַח פֶּסַח הוּא לַיהֹוָה אֲשֶׁר פָּסַח עַל בָּתֵּי בְנֵי יִשְׂרָאֵל בְּמִצְרַיִם בְּנָגְפּוֹ אֶת מִצְרַיִם וְאֶת בָּתֵּינוּ הִצִּיל וַיִּקֹּד הָעָם וַיִּשְׁתַּחֲווּ:

*The Pesach-offering that our fathers ate during the period when the Beit Hamikdash (Holy Temple) stood – what is its reason? Because the Omnipresent passed over the houses of our fathers in Egypt, as it is said: "You shall say, 'It is a*

*Pesach-offering for the Lord because He passed over the houses of the Children of Israel in Egypt, when He struck the Egyptians with a plague, and He saved our houses,' and the people bowed and prostrated themselves."*

### Place your hand on the matzot and say:

Matzöh zo she-önu och'lim al shum
möh. Al shum shelo hispik b'tzekes
shel avo-syanu l'hachamitz ad
she-niglöh alay-hem melech
mal'chay ha-m'löchim ha-ködosh
böruch hu ug'ölöm. Shene-emar
va-yofu es ha-bötzayk asher ho-tzi-u
mimitzra-yim ugos matzos ki lo
chömaytz ki go-r'shu mimitzra-yim
v'lo yöch'lu l'hismah-may-ah v'gam
tzaydöh lo ösu löhem.

מַצָּה זוֹ שֶׁאָנוּ אוֹכְלִים עַל שׁוּם
מָה. עַל שׁוּם שֶׁלֹּא הִסְפִּיק בְּצֵקֶת
שֶׁל אֲבוֹתֵינוּ לְהַחֲמִיץ עַד
שֶׁנִּגְלָה עֲלֵיהֶם מֶלֶךְ
מַלְכֵי הַמְּלָכִים הַקָּדוֹשׁ
בָּרוּךְ הוּא וּגְאָלָם. שֶׁנֶּאֱמַר
וַיֹּאפוּ אֶת הַבָּצֵק אֲשֶׁר הוֹצִיאוּ
מִמִּצְרַיִם עֻגֹת מַצּוֹת כִּי לֹא
חָמֵץ כִּי גֹרְשׁוּ מִמִּצְרַיִם
וְלֹא יָכְלוּ לְהִתְמַהְמֵהַּ וְגַם
צֵדָה לֹא עָשׂוּ לָהֶם:

*This matzah that we eat – what is its reason? Because the dough of our fathers did not have time to rise before the King of kings, the Holy One, blessed be He, revealed Himself to them and redeemed them, as it is said: "They baked the dough that they had brought out of Egypt into matzah cakes, because it had not fermented, for they were driven out of Egypt and could not delay; nor had they prepared any [other] provisions for themselves."*

### Place your hand on the moror and say:

Möror zeh she-önu och'lim al shum    מָרוֹר זֶה שֶׁאָנוּ אוֹכְלִים עַל שׁוּם

78

מָה. עַל שׁוּם שֶׁמְּרָרוּ
הַמִּצְרִים אֶת חַיֵּי אֲבוֹתֵינוּ
בְּמִצְרָיִם. שֶׁנֶּאֱמַר וַיְמָרְרוּ
אֶת חַיֵּיהֶם בַּעֲבֹדָה קָשָׁה
בְּחֹמֶר וּבִלְבֵנִים וּבְכָל עֲבוֹדָה
בַּשָּׂדֶה אֵת כָּל עֲבֹדָתָם אֲשֶׁר
עָבְדוּ בָהֶם בְּפָרֶךְ :

môh. Al shum she-may-r'ru
ha-mitz-rim es cha-yay avosyanu
b'mitzrö-yim. Shene-emar va-y'mö-raru
es cha-yay-hem ba-avodöh köshöh
b'chomer uvil'vaynim uv'chöl avodöh
ba-sö-deh ays köl avodösöm asher
öv'du vöhem b'förech.

*This maror that we eat – what is its reason? Because the Egyptians embittered the lives of our fathers in Egypt, as it is said: "They embittered their lives with harsh labor, with mortar and with bricks, as well as with all kinds of labor in the field; all the toil which they made them serve was with rigor."*

בְּכָל דּוֹר וָדוֹר חַיָּב אָדָם
לִרְאוֹת אֶת עַצְמוֹ כְּאִלּוּ הוּא יָצָא
מִמִּצְרָיִם. שֶׁנֶּאֱמַר וְהִגַּדְתָּ
לְבִנְךָ בַּיוֹם הַהוּא לֵאמֹר בַּעֲבוּר
זֶה עָשָׂה יְהֹוָה לִי בְּצֵאתִי
מִמִּצְרָיִם : לֹא אֶת אֲבוֹתֵינוּ
בִּלְבָד גָּאַל הַקָּדוֹשׁ בָּרוּךְ הוּא
מִמִּצְרָיִם אֶלָּא אַף אוֹתָנוּ גָּאַל
עִמָּהֶם. שֶׁנֶּאֱמַר וְאוֹתָנוּ הוֹצִיא
מִשָּׁם לְמַעַן הָבִיא אוֹתָנוּ לָתֶת
לָנוּ אֶת הָאָרֶץ אֲשֶׁר
נִשְׁבַּע לַאֲבוֹתֵינוּ :

B'chöl dor vödor cha-yöv ödöm
lir-os es atzmo k'ilu hu yö-tzöh
mimitzrö-yim. Shene-emar v'higad-tö
'vin'chö ba-yom ha-hu laymor ba-avur
zeh ösö adonöy li b'tzaysi
mimitzrö-yim. Lo es avo-saynu
bil'vöd gö-al ha-ködosh böruch hu
mimitzra-yim elö af osönu gö-al
imöhem. Shene-emar v'osönu ho-tzi
mishöm l'ma-an hövi osönu löses
lönu es hö-öretz asher
nish-ba la-avosaynu.

79

*In every generation, a person is obligated to regard himself as if he had gone out of Egypt, as it is said: "And you shall tell your son on that day, saying: 'It is because of this that the Lord did for me when I went out of Egypt.' " It was not only our fathers whom the Holy One, blessed be He, redeemed from Egypt; He redeemed us as well, as it is said: "He brought us out from there, so that He might bring us to give us the land He swore to our fathers."*

**Cover the matzot and lift the cup of wine in your hand
for the following paragraph:**

| | |
|---|---|
| L'fichöch anach-nu cha-yövim l'hodos | לְפִיכָךְ אֲנַחְנוּ חַיָּבִים לְהוֹדוֹת |
| l'ha-layl l'shabay-ach l'fö-ayr l'romaym | לְהַלֵּל לְשַׁבֵּחַ לְפָאֵר לְרוֹמֵם |
| l'hadayr l'vöraych l'ayleh ul'kalays, | לְהַדֵּר לְבָרֵךְ לְעַלֵּה וּלְקַלֵּס, |
| l'mi she-ösöh la-avo-saynu v'lönu es | לְמִי שֶׁעָשָׂה לַאֲבוֹתֵינוּ וְלָנוּ אֶת |
| köl ha-nisim hö-aylu, ho-tzi-önu | כָּל הַנִּסִּים הָאֵלּוּ, הוֹצִיאָנוּ |
| may-av'dus l'chay-rus, mi-yögon | מֵעַבְדוּת לְחֵרוּת, מִיָּגוֹן |
| l'simchöh, umay-ayvel l'yom tov, | לְשִׂמְחָה, וּמֵאֵבֶל לְיוֹם טוֹב, |
| umay-afaylöh l'or gödol, umishi-bud | וּמֵאֲפֵלָה לְאוֹר גָּדוֹל, וּמִשִּׁעְבּוּד |
| lig'ulöh, v'nomar l'fönöv ha-l'lu-yöh. | לִגְאֻלָּה, וְנֹאמַר לְפָנָיו הַלְלוּיָהּ: |

*Therefore, we are obliged to thank, praise, laud, glorify, exalt, honor, bless, extol, and acclaim the One Who performed for our fathers and for us all these miracles. He took us out from slavery to freedom, from sorrow to joy, from mourning to festivity, from deep darkness to great light, and from servitude to redemption. Therefore, let us say before Him. Praise the Lord.*

| | |
|---|---|
| Ha-l'lu-yöh, ha-l'lu av'day adonöy, | הַלְלוּיָהּ, הַלְלוּ עַבְדֵי יְהֹוָה, |
| ha-l'lu es shaym adonöy. Y'hi shaym | הַלְלוּ אֶת שֵׁם יְהֹוָה: יְהִי שֵׁם |

adonöy m'voröch, may-atöh v'ad olöm. Mimiz'rach shemesh ad m'vo-o, m'hulöl shaym adonöy. Röm al köl gö-yim adonöy, al ha-shöma-yim k'vodo. Mi ka-donöy elohaynu, ha-magbihi löshöves. Ha-mashpili lir-os, ba-shöma-yim uvö-öretz. M'kimi may-öför döl, may-ash-pos yörim ev'yon. L'hoshivi im n'divim, im n'divay amo. Moshivi akeres ha-ba-yis aym ha-bönim s'maychöh, ha-l'lu-yöh.

יְהֹוָה מְבֹרָךְ, מֵעַתָּה וְעַד עוֹלָם: מִמִּזְרַח שֶׁמֶשׁ עַד מְבוֹאוֹ, מְהֻלָּל שֵׁם יְהֹוָה: רָם עַל כָּל גּוֹיִם יְהֹוָה, עַל הַשָּׁמַיִם כְּבוֹדוֹ: מִי כַּיהֹוָה אֱלֹהֵינוּ, הַמַּגְבִּיהִי לָשָׁבֶת: הַמַּשְׁפִּילִי לִרְאוֹת, בַּשָּׁמַיִם וּבָאָרֶץ: מְקִימִי מֵעָפָר דָּל, מֵאַשְׁפֹּת יָרִים אֶבְיוֹן: לְהוֹשִׁיבִי עִם נְדִיבִים, עִם נְדִיבֵי עַמּוֹ: מוֹשִׁיבִי עֲקֶרֶת הַבַּיִת אֵם הַבָּנִים שְׂמֵחָה, הַלְלוּיָהּ:

*Praise the Lord. Offer praise you servants of the Lord, praise the Name of the Lord. May the Name of the Lord be blessed from now until eternity. From the rising of the sun until its setting, praised is the Name of the Lord. Exalted above all nations is the Lord, above the heavens is His glory. Who is like the Lord, our God, Who dwells on high, yet lowers Himself to look upon the heaven and the earth? He raises the poor from the dust; He lifts the needy from the dunghill, to seat them with nobles, with the nobles of His people. He restores the barren woman into a household, into a joyful mother of children. Praise the Lord.*

B'tzays yisrö-ayl mimitzrö-yim, bays ya-akov may-am lo-ayz. Hö-y'sö y'hudöh l'köd-sho, yisrö-ayl mam-sh'losöv. Ha-yöm rö-öh.

בְּצֵאת יִשְׂרָאֵל מִמִּצְרָיִם, בֵּית יַעֲקֹב מֵעַם לֹעֵז: הָיְתָה יְהוּדָה לְקָדְשׁוֹ, יִשְׂרָאֵל מַמְשְׁלוֹתָיו: הַיָּם רָאָה

| | |
|---|---|
| va-yönos, ha-yardayn yisov l'öchor. | וַיָּנֹס, הַיַּרְדֵּן יִסֹּב לְאָחוֹר: |
| He-hörim rök'du ch'aylim, g'vö-os | הֶהָרִים רָקְדוּ כְאֵילִים, גְּבָעוֹת |
| kiv'nay tzon. Mah l'chö ha-yöm ki | כִּבְנֵי צֹאן: מַה לְּךָ הַיָּם כִּי |
| sönus, ha-yardayn tisov l'öchor. | תָנוּס, הַיַּרְדֵּן תִּסֹּב לְאָחוֹר: |
| Hehörim tir-k'du ch'aylim, g'vö-os | הֶהָרִים תִּרְקְדוּ כְאֵילִים, גְּבָעוֹת |
| kiv'nay tzon. Milif'nay ödon chuli | כִּבְנֵי צֹאן: מִלִּפְנֵי אָדוֹן חוּלִי |
| öretz, milif'nay elo-ah ya-akov. | אָרֶץ, מִלִּפְנֵי אֱלוֹהַּ יַעֲקֹב: |
| Ha-hof'chi ha-tzur agam mö-yim, | הַהֹפְכִי הַצּוּר אֲגַם מָיִם, |
| cha-lömish l'ma-y'no mö-yim. | חַלָּמִישׁ לְמַעְיְנוֹ מָיִם: |

*When Israel went out of Egypt, the House of Yaakov from a people of a alien language, Judah became His holy one, Israel His dominion. The sea saw and fled; the Jordan turned backward. The mountains skipped like rams, the hills like young lambs. What is with you, O sea, that you flee? Jordan, that you turn backward? Mountains, [why] do you skip like rams; hills, like young lambs? [We do so] before the Master, the Creator of the earth, before the God of Yaakov; Who turns the rock into a pool of water, the flintstone into a spring of water.*

**Lift up the cup of wine and say the following two blessings:**

| | |
|---|---|
| Böruch atöh adonöy elohaynu | בָּרוּךְ אַתָּה יְהֹוָה אֱלֹהֵינוּ |
| melech hö-olöm, asher g'ölönu | מֶלֶךְ הָעוֹלָם, אֲשֶׁר גְּאָלָנוּ |
| v'gö-al es avosay-nu mimitzra-yim, | וְגָאַל אֶת אֲבוֹתֵינוּ מִמִּצְרַיִם, |
| vhigi-önu ha-lai-y'löh ha-zeh le-echöl | וְהִגִּיעָנוּ הַלַּיְלָה הַזֶּה לֶאֱכָל |
| bo matzöh umöror, kayn adonöy | בּוֹ מַצָּה וּמָרוֹר, כֵּן יְהֹוָה |
| elohaynu vaylo-hay avosaynu | אֱלֹהֵינוּ וֵאלֹהֵי אֲבוֹתֵינוּ |
| yagi-aynu l'mo-adim v'lir'gölim | יַגִּיעֵנוּ לְמוֹעֲדִים וְלִרְגָלִים |

| | |
|---|---|
| achayrim ha-bö-im lik'rösaynu | אֲחֵרִים הַבָּאִים לִקְרָאתֵנוּ |
| l'shölom s'maychim b'vinyan irechö | לְשָׁלוֹם שְׂמֵחִים בְּבִנְיַן עִירֶךְ |
| v'sösim ba-avodösechö, v'nochal | וְשָׂשִׂים בַּעֲבוֹדָתֶךְ, וְנֹאכַל |
| shöm min ha-z'vöchim umin | שָׁם מִן הַזְּבָחִים וּמִן הַפְּסָחִים |
| hap'söchim (On Shabbat eve: min ha-p'söchim | (במוצאי שבת: מִן הַפְּסָחִים |
| umin ha-z'vöchim) asher yagi-a dömöm al | וּמִן הַזְּבָחִים) אֲשֶׁר יַגִּיעַ דָּמָם עַל |
| kir mizba-chachö l'rö-tzon, v'no-deh | קִיר מִזְבַּחֲךָ לְרָצוֹן, וְנוֹדֶה |
| l'chö shir chödösh al g'ulö-saynu v'al | לְךָ שִׁיר חָדָשׁ עַל גְּאֻלָּתֵנוּ וְעַל |
| p'dus nafshaynu. Böruch atöh | פְּדוּת נַפְשֵׁנוּ: בָּרוּךְ אַתָּה |
| adonöy, gö-al yisrö-ayl. | יְהֹוָה, גָּאַל יִשְׂרָאֵל: |

*Blessed are You, Lord our God, King of the universe, Who redeemed us and redeemed our fathers from Egypt, and Who has enabled us to reach this night so that we may eat matzah and maror. So too, may the Lord our God and God of our fathers enable us to reach other holidays and festivals that will come to us in peace, gladdened in the rebuilding of Your city and rejoicing in Your service. There we shall eat of the sacrifices and of the Pesach-offerings (On Saturday night: of the Pesach-offerings and the sacrifices) whose blood shall be sprinkled on the wall of Your altar to be graciously accepted, and we shall give thanks to You with a new song for our redemption and for the deliverance of our souls. Blessed are You, the Lord Who redeemed Israel.*

| | |
|---|---|
| Böruch atöh adonöy, elohaynu | בָּרוּךְ אַתָּה יְיָ, אֱלֹהֵינוּ |
| melech hö-olöm, boray p'ri ha-göfen. | מֶלֶךְ הָעוֹלָם, בּוֹרֵא פְּרִי הַגָּפֶן: |

*Blessed are You, Lord our God, King of the universe, Who creates the fruit of the vine.*

**Sit and drink the second cup of wine (at least 2 ounces), reclining to the left.**

# • *Rachtzah* •
# Washing the Hands

At this point, everyone washes the hands in the usual prescribed manner of washing before a meal — this time with the customary blessing.

Remove any rings. Fill a large cup with at least 3.5 ounces of cold water, while holding it in your right hand. Transfer the cup to your left hand and pour three times over your whole right hand. Transfer it to your right hand and pour three times over your whole left hand. Rub your hands together and recite the blessing below. Then dry your hands.

Böruch atöh adonöy, elohaynu
melech hö-olöm, asher kid'shönu
b'mitzvosöv, v'tzivönu
al n'tilas yödö-yim.

בָּרוּךְ אַתָּה יְהֹוָה, אֱלֹהֵינוּ
מֶלֶךְ הָעוֹלָם, אֲשֶׁר קִדְּשָׁנוּ
בְּמִצְוֹתָיו, וְצִוָּנוּ
עַל נְטִילַת יָדָיִם :

*Blessed are You, Lord our God, King of the universe, Who has sanctified us with His commandments, and commanded us concerning the washing of the hands.*

---

# • *Motzi Matzah* •
## Eating the Matzah

---

The three matzot are held, the broken one between the two whole ones, and the customary blessing for bread is recited. Then, the bottom matzah is allowed to drop back on the plate, and while holding only the top and middle matzah, the blessing is recited.

**Lift the matzot in the order that they are lying on the seder plate and recite the following blessing:**

בָּרוּךְ אַתָּה יְהֹוָה, אֱלֹהֵינוּ
מֶלֶךְ הָעוֹלָם, הַמּוֹצִיא
לֶחֶם מִן הָאָרֶץ:

Böruch atöh adonöy, elohaynu
melech hö-olöm, ha-mo-tzi
lechem min hö-öretz.

*Blessed are You, the Lord our God, King of the universe, Who brings forth bread from the earth.*

**Let go of the bottom matzah and recite the following blessing (have in mind the *Koreich* Sandwich and the *Afikoman*):**

בָּרוּךְ אַתָּה יְהֹוָה,
אֱלֹהֵינוּ מֶלֶךְ הָעוֹלָם,
אֲשֶׁר קִדְּשָׁנוּ בְּמִצְוֹתָיו,
וְצִוָּנוּ עַל אֲכִילַת מַצָּה:

Böruch atöh adonöy,
elohaynu melech hö-olöm,
asher kid'shönu b'mitzvosöv,
v'tzivönu al achilas matzöh.

*Blessed are You, the Lord our God, King of the universe, Who has sanctified us with His commandments and commanded us concerning the eating of matzah.*

85

For those with their own seder plate, break off at least one ounce from each of the upper and middle matzot (approximatly one handbredth of each) totalling two ounces. Others should eat at least one ounce of matzah (approx. 25.6 grams, or about half of a traditional round matzah). Eat the matzah while reclining to the left.

NOTE: To fulfill one's Biblical obligation to eat matzah one must eat at least one ounce of matzah. It is also important to eat the required amount of matzah within four minutes (the average time of eating a single portion of a meal).

---

## • *Moror* •
## Eating the Bitter Herbs

---

At least 0.75 of an ounce of the bitter herbs are taken and dipped into the *charoset*, and the special blessing is recited. The *moror* is eaten without reclining.

Take a *kezayit* of the *moror* (at least 2 average size leaves of romaine lettuce, and a spoonful of ground horseraddish). Take some *Charoset* and mix some wine into it. Dip the *moror* into the *charoset*. Shake off some of the *charoset* (so that the bitter taste of the *moror* will not be neutralized). When reciting the blessing, bear in mind the *moror* of *koreich* (below).

| | |
|---|---|
| Böruch atöh adonöy elohaynu | בָּרוּךְ אַתָּה יְהוָֹה, אֱלֹהֵינוּ |
| melech hö-olöm, asher kid'shönu | מֶלֶךְ הָעוֹלָם, אֲשֶׁר קִדְּשָׁנוּ |
| b'mitzvosöv, v'tzivönu | בְּמִצְוֹתָיו, וְצִוָּנוּ |
| al achilas möror. | עַל אֲכִילַת מָרוֹר : |

86

*Blessed are You, the Lord our God, King of the universe, Who has sanctified us with His commandments and commanded us concerning the eating of maror.*

Eat the moror without reclining. It is important to eat the required amount of moror within four minutes (the average time of eating a single portion of a meal).

---

## • *Koreich* •
## Eating a Sandwich
## of Matzah and Bitter Herbs

---

In keeping with the custom instituted by Hillel, a great Talmudic sage, a sandwich of matzah and *moror* is made. We recite a special passage and eat the historic "sandwich" while reclining.

Take the bottom matzah and break it in half. Form a "sandwich" by placing some *moror* (at least 2 average size leaves of romaine lettuce, and a spoonful of ground horseraddish) between the two pieces. Dip the *moror* into the *charoset*. Shake off some of the *charoset*. Recite the passage below:

| | |
|---|---|
| Kayn ösö hi-lel hilayl biz'man | כֵּן עָשָׂה הִלֵּל בִּזְמַן |
| she-bays ha-mikdösh hö-yöh | שֶׁבֵּית הַמִּקְדָּשׁ הָיָה |
| koraych pesach matzöh umöror | קַיָּם הָיָה כּוֹרֵךְ פֶּסַח מַצָּה וּמָרוֹר |
| v'ochayl b'yachad, k'mo shene-emar | וְאוֹכֵל בְּיַחַד, כְּמוֹ שֶׁנֶּאֱמַר |
| al matzos um'rorim yoch'luhu. | עַל מַצּוֹת וּמְרוֹרִים יֹאכְלֻהוּ׃ |

*Thus did Hillel at the time when the Beit Hamikdash (Holy Temple) was standing; He would combine the Pesach-offering, matzah, and maror and eat them together, as it is said: "with matzot and maror they shall eat it."*

Eat the "sandwich" while reclining to the left. It is important to eat the sandwich within four minutes (the average time of eating a single portion of a meal).

---

## • *Shulchan Oraych* •
# The Festive Feast

---

The holiday meal is served. It is customary to begin the festive meal by eating the egg from the seder plate, after it is dipped in salt-water, to recall the *Chagigah* (Festival) sacrifice offered in the *Beit Hamikdash* (Holy Temple). Note: The *Zero'a* (chicken neck) from the seder plate is not eaten, as it is only a "remembrance" of the Paschal lamb.

Care should be taken during the meal to avoid having matzah come in contact with water, as minute amounts of unbaked flour may be present and become leavened. For this reason the matzot on the table are best kept covered or in plastic bags (Ziploc™, etc.). Wine can be served during the meal.

# • *Tzofun* •
# The *Afikoman*

After the meal, the half matzah that had been set aside ("hidden") for the *Afikoman*, is taken out and eaten. It symbolizes the Paschal lamb that was eaten at the end of the meal in Temple times, together with matzah. During the first seder the *Afikoman* should be eaten before midnight.

After eating the *Afikoman* one should not eat or drink anything except for the two remaining cups of wine (and if necessary, water), so that the taste of the matzah will remain in the mouth.

Take at least two ounces of matzah, including some from the *Afikoman*. Eat the matzah while reclining to the left. It is important to eat the *Afikoman* within four minutes (the average time of eating a single portion of a meal).

# • *Bairach* •
## Grace After the Meal

Following the meal we give thanks to God for the nourishment He provided. A third cup of wine is filled and the Grace After Meals is recited. After reciting the Grace we recite a blessing on the wine and drink the third cup. These prefatory psalms set the tone for the Grace to follow.

Fill the third cup of wine, and another cup for the "Cup of Elijah," which is usually placed in the center of the table.

| | |
|---|---|
| Shir ha-ma-alos, b'shuv adonöy es | שִׁיר הַמַּעֲלוֹת, בְּשׁוּב יְהֹוָה אֶת |
| shivas tziyon hö-yinu k'chol'mim. | שִׁיבַת צִיּוֹן הָיִינוּ כְּחֹלְמִים: |
| Öz yimölay s'chok pinu | אָז יִמָּלֵא שְׂחוֹק פִּינוּ |
| ul'shonaynu rinöh, öz yom'ru | וּלְשׁוֹנֵנוּ רִנָּה, אָז יֹאמְרוּ |
| vago-yim higdil adonöy la-asos im | בַגּוֹיִם הִגְדִּיל יְהֹוָה לַעֲשׂוֹת עִם |
| ay-leh. Higdil adonöy la-asos | אֵלֶּה: הִגְדִּיל יְהֹוָה לַעֲשׂוֹת |
| imönu, hö-yinu s'maychim. | עִמָּנוּ, הָיִינוּ שְׂמֵחִים: |
| Shuvöh adonöy es sh'visaynu, | שׁוּבָה יְהֹוָה אֶת שְׁבִיתֵנוּ, |
| ka-afikim banegev. Ha-zor'im | כַּאֲפִיקִים בַּנֶּגֶב: הַזֹּרְעִים |
| b'dim-öh b'rinöh yiktzoru. | בְּדִמְעָה בְּרִנָּה יִקְצֹרוּ: |
| Höloch yaylaych uvöchoh | הָלוֹךְ יֵלֵךְ וּבָכֹה |
| nosay meshech ha-zöra, bo yövo | נֹשֵׂא מֶשֶׁךְ הַזָּרַע, בֹּא יָבֹא |
| v'rinöh nosay alumosöv. | בְרִנָּה נֹשֵׂא אֲלֻמֹּתָיו: |

90

*A Song of Ascents. When the Lord will return the exiles of Zion, we will have been like dreamers. Then our mouth will be filled with laughter, and our tongue with songs of joy; then will they say among the nations, "The Lord has done great things for these." The Lord has done great things for us; we were joyful. Lord, return our exiles as streams to arid soil. Those who sow in tears will reap with songs of joy. He goes along weeping, carrying the bag of seed; he will surely return with songs of joy, carrying his sheaves.*

| | |
|---|---|
| Liv'nay korach mizmor shir, | לִבְנֵי קֹרַח מִזְמוֹר שִׁיר, |
| y'sudöso b'har'ray kodesh. Ohayv | יְסוּדָתוֹ בְּהַרְרֵי קֹדֶשׁ: אֹהֵב |
| adonöy sha-aray tziyon mi-kol | יְהֹוָה שַׁעֲרֵי צִיּוֹן, מִכֹּל |
| mish-k'nos ya-akov. Nichbödos | מִשְׁכְּנוֹת יַעֲקֹב: נִכְבָּדוֹת |
| m'dubör böch, ir hö-elohim selöh. | מְדֻבָּר בָּךְ, עִיר הָאֱלֹהִים סֶלָה: |
| Azkir rahav uvövel l'yo-d'öy, | אַזְכִּיר רַהַב וּבָבֶל לְיֹדְעָי, |
| hinay f'leshes v'tzor im kush zeh | הִנֵּה פְלֶשֶׁת וְצוֹר עִם כּוּשׁ זֶה |
| yulad shöm. Ul'tziyon yay-ömar ish | יֻלַּד שָׁם: וּלְצִיּוֹן יֵאָמַר אִישׁ |
| v'ish yulad böh v'hu y'cho-n'nehö | וְאִישׁ יֻלַּד בָּהּ, וְהוּא יְכוֹנְנֶהָ |
| el-yon. Adonöy yispor bich'sov | עֶלְיוֹן: יְהֹוָה יִסְפֹּר בִּכְתוֹב |
| amim, zeh yulad shöm selöh. | עַמִּים, זֶה יֻלַּד שָׁם סֶלָה: |
| V'shörim k'chol-lim, kol | וְשָׁרִים כְּחֹלְלִים, כֹּל |
| ma-yönai böch. | מַעְיָנַי בָּךְ: |

*By the sons of Korach, a Psalm, a Song whose basic theme is the holy mountains [of Zion and Jerusalem]. The Lord loves the gates of Zion more than all the dwelling places of Jacob. Glorious things are spoken of you, eternal city of God. I will remind Rahav and Babylon concerning my beloved; Philistia and Tyre as well as Ethiopia, "This one was born there." And to Zion will be said, "This person and that was born there"; and He, the Most High, will establish it. The Lord will count in the register of people, "This one was born there." Selah. Singers as well as dancers [will sing your praise and say], "All my inner thoughts are of you."*

| | |
|---|---|
| Avö-r'chöh es adonöy b'chöl ays, | אֲבָרְכָה אֶת יְהֹוָה בְּכָל עֵת, |
| tömid t'hilöso b'fi. Sof dövör | תָּמִיד תְּהִלָּתוֹ בְּפִי : סוֹף דָּבָר |
| ha-kol nishmö, es hö-elohim y'rö | הַכֹּל נִשְׁמָע, אֶת הָאֱלֹהִים יְרָא |
| v'es mitzvosöv sh'mor ki zeh köl | וְאֶת מִצְוֹתָיו שְׁמוֹר כִּי זֶה כָּל |
| hö-ödöm. T'hilas adonöy y'daber pi, | הָאָדָם : תְּהִלַּת יְהֹוָה יְדַבֶּר פִּי, |
| vivö-raych kol bösör shaym köd-sho | וִיבָרֵךְ כָּל בָּשָׂר שֵׁם קָדְשׁוֹ |
| l'olöm vö-ed. Va-anachnu n'vöraych | לְעוֹלָם וָעֶד : וַאֲנַחְנוּ נְבָרֵךְ |
| yöh, may-atöh v'ad olöm, ha-l'luyöh. | יָהּ, מֵעַתָּה וְעַד עוֹלָם, הַלְלוּיָהּ : |

*I will bless the Lord at all times; His praise is always in my mouth. Ultimately, all is known: Fear God, and observe His commandments; for this is the whole purpose of man. My mouth will utter the praise of the Lord; let all flesh bless His holy Name forever. And we will bless the Lord from now to eternity. Praise the Lord.*

**The *Mayim Acharonim*, washing of the fingertips, is performed prior to the Grace After a Meal.**

Pour some water into a small cup. Pour a little over the fingertips of both hands into a bowl. Remove the bowl from the table.

| | |
|---|---|
| **Before washing the fingertips, say:** | קוֹדֶם מַיִם אַחֲרוֹנִים יֹאמַר : |
| Zeh chaylek ödöm röshö | זֶה חֵלֶק אָדָם רָשָׁע |
| may-elohim v'nachalas imro may-ayl. | מֵאֱלֹהִים וְנַחֲלַת אִמְרוֹ מֵאֵל : |

After washing the fingertips, say: אחר מים אחרונים יאמר :

Va-y'dabayr aylai zeh ha-shulchön וַיְדַבֵּר אֵלַי זֶה הַשֻּׁלְחָן

asher lif'nay adonöy. אֲשֶׁר לִפְנֵי יְיָ :

*This is the portion of a wicked man from God, and the heritage assigned to him by God. And he said to me: This is the table that is before the Lord.*

If three or more male adults are present the following Call to Grace is said. Otherwise, proceed on page 94.

The leader begins: אם מברכים בזימון אומר המברך :

Rabo-sai mir vel'n ben-tsh'n. רַבּוֹתַי מִיר וֶועֶלִין בֶּעְנְטְשִׁין :

The others answer: ועונין המסובין :

Y'hi shaym adonöy m'voröch יְהִי שֵׁם יְיָ מְבֹרָךְ

may-atöh v'ad olöm. מֵעַתָּה וְעַד עוֹלָם :

The leader continues: המברך אומר :

Y'hi shaym adonöy m'voröch יְהִי שֵׁם יְיָ מְבֹרָךְ

may-atöh v'ad olöm. מֵעַתָּה וְעַד עוֹלָם :

Bir'shus mö-rönön בִּרְשׁוּת מָרָנָן

v'ra-bönön v'ra-bosai n'vö-raych... וְרַבָּנָן וְרַבּוֹתַי נְבָרֵךְ

With 10 men add: Elohaynu... (ואם הם עשרה :... אֱלֹהֵינוּ...)

Otherwise continue: שֶׁאָכַלְנוּ מִשֶּׁלּוֹ :

...she-öchalnu mi-shelo. ועונין המסובין,

The others answer, followed by the leader: ואחריהם המברך :

Böruch (elohaynu) she-öchalnu בָּרוּךְ (אֱלֹהֵינוּ)

mi-shelo uv'tuvo chö-yinu שֶׁאָכַלְנוּ מִשֶּׁלּוֹ וּבְטוּבוֹ חָיִינוּ :

*Gentlemen, let us say the blessings. May the name of the Lord be blessed from now*

93

*and to all eternity. With your permission, esteemed gentlemen, let us bless Him (If at least ten men are present: our God,) of Whose bounty we have eaten. Blessed be He (If at least ten men are present: our God,) of Whose bounty we have eaten and by Whose goodness we live.*

**Lift the cup of wine with your right hand. Transfer it to the left hand. Lower it into the cupped palm of your right hand (if you write with your left hand, reverse). Lift the cup at least 3 inches above the table (through page 100) and recite below.**

| | |
|---|---|
| Böruch atöh adonöy elohaynu | בָּרוּךְ אַתָּה יְהֹוָה אֱלֹהֵינוּ |
| melech hö-olöm, ha-zön es hö-olöm | מֶלֶךְ הָעוֹלָם, הַזָּן אֶת הָעוֹלָם |
| kulo b'tuvo b'chayn b'chesed | כֻּלּוֹ בְּטוּבוֹ בְּחֵן בְּחֶסֶד |
| uv'rachamim, hu nosayn lechem | וּבְרַחֲמִים הוּא נוֹתֵן לֶחֶם |
| l'chöl bösör, ki l'olöm chasdo. | לְכָל בָּשָׂר, כִּי לְעוֹלָם חַסְדּוֹ: |
| Uv'tuvo ha-gödol imönu tömid lo | וּבְטוּבוֹ הַגָּדוֹל עִמָּנוּ תָּמִיד לֹא |
| chösayr lönu v'al yechsar lönu | חָסֵר לָנוּ וְאַל יֶחְסַר לָנוּ |
| mözon l'olöm vö-ed. Ba-avur sh'mo | מָזוֹן לְעוֹלָם וָעֶד: בַּעֲבוּר שְׁמוֹ |
| ha-gödol, ki hu ayl zön um'farnays | הַגָּדוֹל, כִּי הוּא אֵל זָן וּמְפַרְנֵס |
| lakol umaytiv lakol umaychin | לַכֹּל וּמֵטִיב לַכֹּל וּמֵכִין |
| mözon l'chöl b'riyosöv asher börö, | מָזוֹן לְכָל בְּרִיּוֹתָיו אֲשֶׁר בָּרָא, |
| kö-ömur, posay-ach es yödechö | כָּאָמוּר, פּוֹתֵחַ אֶת יָדֶךְ |
| u-masbi-a l'chöl chai rötzon. | וּמַשְׂבִּיעַ לְכָל חַי רָצוֹן: |
| Böruch atöh adonöy, | בָּרוּךְ אַתָּה יְיָ, |
| hazön es ha-kol. | הַזָּן אֶת הַכֹּל: |

*Blessed are You, Lord our God, King of the universe, Who, in His goodness,* '
*provides sustenance for the entire world with grace, with kindness and with mercy.*
*He gives food to all flesh, for His kindness is everlasting. Through His great*

*goodness to us continuously we do not lack [food], and may we never lack food, for the sake of His great Name. For He, benevolent God, provides nourishment and sustenance for all, does good to all, and prepares food for all His creatures whom He has created, as it is said: You open Your hand and satisfy the desire of every living thing. Blessed are You Lord, Who provides food for all.*

| | |
|---|---|
| No-deh l'chö adonöy elohaynu al | נוֹדֶה לְךָ יְהֹוָה אֱלֹהֵינוּ עַל |
| shehin-chaltö la-avosaynu eretz | שֶׁהִנְחַלְתָּ לַאֲבוֹתֵינוּ אֶרֶץ |
| chemdöh tovöh ur'chövöh, v'al | חֶמְדָּה טוֹבָה וּרְחָבָה, וְעַל |
| she-ho-tzay-sönu adonöy elohaynu | שֶׁהוֹצֵאתָנוּ יְהֹוָה אֱלֹהֵינוּ |
| may-eretz mitzra-yim uf'disönu | מֵאֶרֶץ מִצְרַיִם וּפְדִיתָנוּ |
| mibays avödim, v'al | מִבֵּית עֲבָדִים, וְעַל |
| b'ris'chö shechö-samtö biv'söraynu | בְּרִיתְךָ שֶׁחָתַמְתָּ בִּבְשָׂרֵנוּ |
| v'al torös'chö shelimad-tönu | וְעַל תּוֹרָתְךָ שֶׁלִּמַּדְתָּנוּ |
| v'al chukechö shehoda-tönu | וְעַל חֻקֶּיךָ שֶׁהוֹדַעְתָּנוּ |
| v'al cha-yim chayn vöchesed | וְעַל חַיִּים חֵן וָחֶסֶד |
| she-chonantönu v'al achilas mözon | שֶׁחוֹנַנְתָּנוּ וְעַל אֲכִילַת מָזוֹן |
| shö-atöh zön um'farnays osönu | שָׁאַתָּה זָן וּמְפַרְנֵס אוֹתָנוּ |
| tömid b'chöl yom uv'chöl | תָּמִיד בְּכָל יוֹם וּבְכָל |
| ays uv'chöl shö-öh. | עֵת וּבְכָל שָׁעָה: |

*We offer thanks to You, Lord our God, for having given as a heritage to our ancestors a precious, good and spacious land; for having brought us out, Lord our God, from the land of Egypt and redeemed us from the house of bondage; for Your covenant which You have sealed in our flesh; for Your Torah which You have taught us; for Your statutes which You have made known to us; for the life, favor and kindness which You have graciously bestowed upon us; and for the food we eat with which You constantly nourish and sustain us every day, at all times, and at every hour.*

V'al ha-kol adonöy elohaynu    וְעַל הַכֹּל יְהֹוָה אֱלֹהֵינוּ

anachnu modim löch um'vö-r'chim    אֲנַחְנוּ מוֹדִים לָךְ וּמְבָרְכִים

osöch yisböraych shim'chö b'fi köl    אוֹתָךְ יִתְבָּרֵךְ שִׁמְךָ בְּפִי כָּל

chai tömid l'olöm vö-ed. Kakösuv,    חַי תָּמִיד לְעוֹלָם וָעֶד : כַּכָּתוּב,

v'öchaltö v'sövö-tö uvayrachtö es    וְאָכַלְתָּ וְשָׂבָעְתָּ וּבֵרַכְתָּ אֶת

adonöy elohechö al hö-öretz    יְהֹוָה אֱלֹהֶיךָ עַל הָאָרֶץ

ha-tovöh asher nösan löch.    הַטֹּבָה אֲשֶׁר נָתַן לָךְ.

Böruch atöh adonöy,    בָּרוּךְ אַתָּה יְיָ,

al hö-öretz v'al ha-mözon.    עַל הָאָרֶץ וְעַל הַמָּזוֹן :

*For all this, Lord our God, we give thanks to You and bless You. May Your Name be blessed by the mouth of every living being, constantly and forever. As it is written: When you have eaten and are satiated, you shall bless the Lord your God for the good land which He has given you. Blessed are You Lord, for the land and for the sustenance.*

Rachaym adonöy elohaynu    רַחֵם יְהֹוָה אֱלֹהֵינוּ

al yisrö-ayl amechö v'al    עַל יִשְׂרָאֵל עַמֶּךָ וְעַל

y'rushöla-yim irechö v'al tziyon    יְרוּשָׁלַיִם עִירֶךָ וְעַל צִיּוֹן

mishkan k'vodechö v'al mal'chus    מִשְׁכַּן כְּבוֹדֶךָ וְעַל מַלְכוּת

bays dövid m'shichechö v'al    בֵּית דָּוִד מְשִׁיחֶךָ וְעַל

haba-yis ha-gödol v'haködosh    הַבַּיִת הַגָּדוֹל וְהַקָּדוֹשׁ

shenikrö shim'chö ölöv. Elohaynu שֶׁנִּקְרָא שִׁמְךָ עָלָיו : אֱלֹהֵינוּ
övinu ro-aynu zonaynu parn'saynu אָבִינוּ רוֹעֵנוּ זוֹנֵנוּ פַּרְנְסֵנוּ
v'chal-k'laynu v'harvi-chaynu וְכַלְכְּלֵנוּ וְהַרְוִיחֵנוּ
v'harvach lönu adonöy elohaynu וְהַרְוַח לָנוּ יְהֹוָה אֱלֹהֵינוּ
m'hayröh miköl tzörosaynu. V'nö al מְהֵרָה מִכָּל צָרוֹתֵינוּ : וְנָא אַל
tatz-richaynu adonöy elohaynu, תַּצְרִיכֵנוּ יְהֹוָה אֱלֹהֵינוּ,
lo liday mat'nas bösör vödöm v'lo לֹא לִידֵי מַתְּנַת בָּשָׂר וָדָם וְלֹא
liday ha-lvö-ösöm ki im l'yöd'chö לִידֵי הַלְוָאָתָם כִּי אִם לְיָדְךָ
ham'lay-öh ha-p'suchöh ha-k'doshöh הַמְּלֵאָה הַפְּתוּחָה הַקְּדוֹשָׁה
v'hör'chövöh shelo nayvosh v'lo וְהָרְחָבָה שֶׁלֹּא נֵבוֹשׁ וְלֹא
niкölaym l'olöm vö-ed. נִכָּלֵם לְעוֹלָם וָעֶד :

*Have mercy, Lord our God, upon Israel Your people, upon Jerusalem Your city, upon Zion the abode of Your glory, upon the kingship of the house of David Your anointed, and upon the great and holy House over which Your Name was proclaimed. Our God, our Father, tend us, nourish us, sustain us, feed us and provide us with plenty, and speedily, Lord our God, grant us relief from all our afflictions. Lord our God, please do not make us dependent upon the gifts of mortal men nor upon their loans, but only upon Your full, open, holy and generous hand, that we may never be shamed or disgraced.*

---

**On Shabbat:** בשבת :

R'tzay v'hachali-tzaynu adonöy רְצֵה וְהַחֲלִיצֵנוּ יְיָ
elohaynu b'mitzvosechö uv'mitzvas אֱלֹהֵינוּ בְּמִצְוֹתֶיךָ וּבְמִצְוַת

| | |
|---|---|
| yom ha-sh'vi-i ha-shabbös ha-gödol | יוֹם הַשְּׁבִיעִי הַשַּׁבָּת הַגָּדוֹל |
| v'haködosh ha-zeh ki yom zeh | וְהַקָּדוֹשׁ הַזֶּה כִּי יוֹם זֶה |
| gödol v'ködosh hu l'fönechö, | גָּדוֹל וְקָדוֹשׁ הוּא לְפָנֶיךָ, |
| lishbös bo v'lönu-ach bo b'ahavöh | לִשְׁבָּת בּוֹ וְלָנוּחַ בּוֹ בְּאַהֲבָה |
| k'mitzvas r'tzonechö, uvir'tzon'chö | כְּמִצְוַת רְצוֹנֶךָ, וּבִרְצוֹנְךָ |
| höni-ach lönu adonöy elohaynu | הָנִיחַ לָנוּ יְהֹוָה אֱלֹהֵינוּ |
| shelo s'hay tzöröh v'yögon | שֶׁלֹּא תְהֵא צָרָה וְיָגוֹן |
| va-anöchöh b'yom m'nuchösaynu, | וַאֲנָחָה בְּיוֹם מְנוּחָתֵנוּ, |
| v'har-aynu adonöy elohaynu | וְהַרְאֵנוּ יְהֹוָה אֱלֹהֵינוּ |
| b'nechömas tziyon irechö, | בְּנֶחָמַת צִיּוֹן עִירֶךָ, |
| uv'vinyan y'rushöla-yim ir | וּבְבִנְיַן יְרוּשָׁלַיִם עִיר |
| köd-shechö, ki atöh hu ba-al | קָדְשֶׁךָ, כִּי אַתָּה הוּא בַּעַל |
| ha-y'shu-os uva-al ha-nechömos. | הַיְשׁוּעוֹת וּבַעַל הַנֶּחָמוֹת׃ |

*May it please You, Lord our God, to strengthen us through Your mitzvot, and through the mitzvah of the Seventh Day, this great and holy Shabbat. For this day is great and holy before You, to refrain from work and to rest thereon with love, in accordance with the commandment of Your will. In Your good will, Lord our God, bestow upon us tranquility, that there shall be no distress, sadness or sorrow on the day of our rest. Lord our God, let us see the consolation of Zion Your city, and the rebuilding of Jerusalem Your holy city, for You are the Master of deliverance and the Master of consolation.*

### Continue here:

| | |
|---|---|
| Elohaynu vay-lohay avo-saynu | אֱלֹהֵינוּ וֵאלֹהֵי אֲבוֹתֵינוּ |
| ya-aleh v'yövo, v'yagi-a v'yayrö-eh | יַעֲלֶה וְיָבֹא, וְיַגִּיעַ וְיֵרָאֶה |

| | |
|---|---|
| v'yayrö-tzeh, v'yishöma v'yipökayd | וְיֵרָצֶה, וְיִשָּׁמַע וְיִפָּקֵד |
| v'yizöchayr, zichro-naynu | וְיִזָּכֵר, זִכְרוֹנֵנוּ |
| ufik'do-naynu, v'zichron | וּפִקְדוֹנֵנוּ, וְזִכְרוֹן |
| avosaynu, v'zichron möshi-ach | אֲבוֹתֵינוּ, וְזִכְרוֹן מָשִׁיחַ |
| ben dövid avdechö, v'zichron | בֶּן דָּוִד עַבְדֶּךָ, וְזִכְרוֹן |
| y'rushöla-yim ir köd-shechö, | יְרוּשָׁלַיִם עִיר קָדְשֶׁךָ, |
| v'zichron köl am'chö bays yisrö-ayl | וְזִכְרוֹן כָּל עַמְּךָ בֵּית יִשְׂרָאֵל |
| l'fönechö lif'laytöh l'tovöh, l'chayn | לְפָנֶיךָ לִפְלֵיטָה לְטוֹבָה, לְחֵן |
| ul'chesed ul'rachamim ul'cha-yim | וּלְחֶסֶד וּלְרַחֲמִים וּלְחַיִּים |
| tovim ul'shölom b'yom chag | טוֹבִים וּלְשָׁלוֹם, בְּיוֹם חַג |
| ha-matzos ha-zeh, b'yom tov mikrö | הַמַּצּוֹת הַזֶּה, בְּיוֹם טוֹב מִקְרָא |
| kodesh ha-zeh. Zöch'raynu adonöy | קֹדֶשׁ הַזֶּה. זָכְרֵנוּ יְיָ |
| elohaynu bo l'tovöh, ufök'daynu vo | אֱלֹהֵינוּ בּוֹ לְטוֹבָה, וּפָקְדֵנוּ בוֹ |
| liv'röchöh, v'hoshi-aynu vo l'cha-yim | לִבְרָכָה, וְהוֹשִׁיעֵנוּ בוֹ לְחַיִּים |
| tovim. uvid'var y'shu-öh v'rachamim | טוֹבִים: וּבִדְבַר יְשׁוּעָה וְרַחֲמִים |
| chus v'chönaynu v'rachaym ölaynu | חוּס וְחָנֵּנוּ וְרַחֵם עָלֵינוּ |
| v'hoshi-aynu ki aylechö aynaynu, | וְהוֹשִׁיעֵנוּ כִּי אֵלֶיךָ עֵינֵינוּ, |
| ki ayl melech chanun | כִּי אֵל מֶלֶךְ חַנּוּן |
| v'rachum ötöh. | וְרַחוּם אָתָּה: |

*Our God and God of our fathers, may there ascend, come and reach, be seen, accepted, and heard, recalled and remembered before You, the remembrance and recollection of us, the remembrance of our fathers, the remembrance of Moshiach the son of David Your servant, the remembrance of Jerusalem Your holy city, and the remembrance of all Your people the House of Israel, for deliverance, well-being, grace, kindness, mercy, good life and peace, on this day of the Festival of Matzot, on this holy Festival day. Remember us on this [day], Lord our God, for good; be mindful of us on this [day] for blessing; help us on this [day] for good life. With the promise of deliverance and compassion, spare us and be gracious to us; have mercy upon us and deliver us; for our eyes are directed to You, for You, God, are a gracious and merciful King.*

| | |
|---|---|
| Uv'nay y'rushöla-yim ir ha-kodesh | וּבְנֵה יְרוּשָׁלַיִם עִיר הַקֹּדֶשׁ |
| bim'hayröh v'yömaynu. Böruch atöh | בִּמְהֵרָה בְיָמֵינוּ. בָּרוּךְ |
| adonöy, bonay v'rachamöv | אַתָּה יְהֹוָה, בֹּנֵה בְרַחֲמָיו |
| y'rushölö-yim. Ömayn. | יְרוּשָׁלָיִם. אָמֵן : |

*And rebuild Jerusalem the holy city speedily in our days. Blessed are You Lord, Who in His mercy rebuilds Jerusalem. Amen.*

**Return the cup of wine to the table and continue below:**

| | |
|---|---|
| Boruch atöh adonöy elohaynu | בָּרוּךְ אַתָּה יְהֹוָה אֱלֹהֵינוּ |
| melech hö-olöm, hö-ayl, övinu | מֶלֶךְ הָעוֹלָם, הָאֵל, אָבִינוּ |
| malkaynu, adiraynu bor'aynu | מַלְכֵּנוּ, אַדִּירֵנוּ בּוֹרְאֵנוּ |
| go-alaynu yo-tz'raynu, k'doshaynu | גֹּאֲלֵנוּ יוֹצְרֵנוּ, קְדוֹשֵׁנוּ |
| k'dosh ya-akov ro-aynu ro-ay | קְדוֹשׁ יַעֲקֹב רוֹעֵנוּ רוֹעֵה |
| yisrö-ayl ha-melech ha-tov | יִשְׂרָאֵל הַמֶּלֶךְ הַטּוֹב |
| v'hamaytiv lakol b'chöl yom | וְהַמֵּטִיב לַכֹּל בְּכָל יוֹם |
| vö-yom, hu haytiv lönu, hu | וָיוֹם, הוּא הֵיטִיב לָנוּ, הוּא |
| maytiv lönu, hu yaytiv lönu, | מֵטִיב לָנוּ, הוּא יֵיטִיב לָנוּ, |
| hu g'mölönu hu gom'laynu | הוּא גְמָלָנוּ הוּא גוֹמְלֵנוּ |

| | |
|---|---|
| hu yig-m'laynu lö-ad, l'chayn | הוּא יִגְמְלֵנוּ לָעַד, לְחֵן |
| ul'chesed ul'rachamim, ul'revach | וּלְחֶסֶד וּלְרַחֲמִים, וּלְרֶוַח |
| hatzölöh v'hatzlöchöh, b'röchöh | הַצָּלָה וְהַצְלָחָה, בְּרָכָה |
| vishu-öh, nechömöh parnösöh | וִישׁוּעָה, נֶחָמָה פַּרְנָסָה |
| v'chalkölöh v'rachamim v'cha-yim | וְכַלְכָּלָה וְרַחֲמִים וְחַיִּים |
| v'shölom v'chöl tov umiköl | וְשָׁלוֹם וְכָל טוֹב וּמִכָּל |
| tuv l'olöm al y'chas'raynu. | טוּב לְעוֹלָם אַל יְחַסְּרֵנוּ: |

*Blessed are You, Lord our God, King of the universe, benevolent God, our Father, our King, our Strength, our Creator, our Redeemer, our Maker, our Holy One, the Holy One of Jacob, our Shepherd, the Shepherd of Israel, the King Who is good and does good to all, each and every day. He has done good for us, He does good for us, and He will do good for us; He has bestowed, He bestows, and He will forever bestow upon us grace, kindness and mercy, relief, salvation and success, blessing and deliverance, consolation, livelihood and sustenance, compassion, life, peace and all goodness; and may He never cause us to lack any good.*

| | |
|---|---|
| Hörachamön hu yimloch ölaynu | הָרַחֲמָן הוּא יִמְלוֹךְ עָלֵינוּ |
| l'olöm vö-ed. Hörachamön hu | לְעוֹלָם וָעֶד: הָרַחֲמָן הוּא |
| yisböraych bashöma-yim | יִתְבָּרֵךְ בַּשָּׁמַיִם |
| u-vö-öretz. Hörachamön hu | וּבָאָרֶץ: הָרַחֲמָן הוּא |
| yishtabach l'dor dorim v'yispö-ayr | יִשְׁתַּבַּח לְדוֹר דּוֹרִים וְיִתְפָּאֵר |
| bönu lö-ad ul'nay-tzach n'tzöchim | בָּנוּ לָעַד וּלְנֵצַח נְצָחִים |
| v'yis-hadar bönu lö-ad ul'ol'may | וְיִתְהַדַּר בָּנוּ לָעַד וּלְעוֹלְמֵי |
| olömim. Hörachamön hu | עוֹלָמִים: הָרַחֲמָן הוּא |

y'far-n'saynu b'chövod.

Hörachamön hu yishbor ol gölus
may-al tzavöraynu v'hu yolichaynu
ko-m'miyus l'ar-tzaynu.

Hörachamön hu yishlach b'röchöh
m'ruböh b'va-yis zeh v'al shul-chön
zeh she-öchalnu ölöv. Hörachamön
hu yishlach lönu es ayli-yöhu
ha-növi zöchur latov, vivaser lönu
b'soros tovos y'shu-os v'nechömos.

Hörachamön hu y'vöraych es övi
mori ba-al ha-ba-yis ha-zeh v'es imi
morösi ba-las ha-ba-yis ha-zeh,
osöm v'es baysöm v'es zar-öm v'es
köl asher löhem, osönu v'es köl
asher lönu. K'mo shebayrach es
avosaynu avröhöm yitz-chök
v'ya-akov bakol mikol kol, kayn
y'vöraych osönu (b'nay v'ris) kulönu
yachad biv'röchöh sh'laymöh
v'nomar ömayn.

יְפַרְנְסֵנוּ בְּכָבוֹד :
הָרַחֲמָן הוּא יִשְׁבּוֹר עוֹל גָּלוּת
מֵעַל צַוָּארֵנוּ וְהוּא יוֹלִיכֵנוּ
קוֹמְמִיּוּת לְאַרְצֵנוּ :
הָרַחֲמָן הוּא יִשְׁלַח בְּרָכָה
מְרֻבָּה בְּבַיִת זֶה וְעַל שֻׁלְחָן
זֶה שֶׁאָכַלְנוּ עָלָיו : הָרַחֲמָן
הוּא יִשְׁלַח לָנוּ אֶת אֵלִיָּהוּ
הַנָּבִיא זָכוּר לַטּוֹב, וִיבַשֶּׂר לָנוּ
בְּשׂוֹרוֹת טוֹבוֹת יְשׁוּעוֹת וְנֶחָמוֹת :
הָרַחֲמָן הוּא יְבָרֵךְ אֶת אָבִי
מוֹרִי בַּעַל הַבַּיִת הַזֶּה וְאֶת אִמִּי
מוֹרָתִי בַּעֲלַת הַבַּיִת הַזֶּה,
אוֹתָם וְאֶת בֵּיתָם וְאֶת זַרְעָם וְאֶת
כָּל אֲשֶׁר לָהֶם, אוֹתָנוּ וְאֶת כָּל
אֲשֶׁר לָנוּ : כְּמוֹ שֶׁבֵּרַךְ אֶת
אֲבוֹתֵינוּ אַבְרָהָם יִצְחָק
וְיַעֲקֹב בַּכֹּל מִכֹּל כֹּל, כֵּן
יְבָרֵךְ אוֹתָנוּ (בני ברית) כֻּלָּנוּ
יַחַד בִּבְרָכָה שְׁלֵמָה
וְנֹאמַר אָמֵן :

*May the Merciful One reign over us forever and ever. May the Merciful One be blessed in heaven and on earth. May the Merciful One be praised for all generations, and pride Himself in us forever and all eternity, and glorify Himself* in us forever and ever. May the Merciful One provide our livelihood with honor. May the Merciful One break the yoke of exile from our neck and may He lead us upright to our land. May the Merciful One send abundant blessing into this house and upon this table at which we have eaten. May the Merciful One send us Elijah the prophet — may he be remembered for good — and let him bring us good tidings, deliverance and consolation. (May the Merciful One bless our master, our teacher, and our leader.) May the Merciful One bless my father, my teacher, the master of this house, and my mother, my teacher, the mistress of this house; them, their household, their children, and all that is theirs; us, and all that is ours. Just as He blessed our forefathers, Abraham, Isaac and Jacob, "in all things," "by all things," with "all things," so may He bless all of us together (the children of the Covenant) with a perfect blessing, and let us say, Amen.

| | |
|---|---|
| Mimörom y'lam'du ölöv v'ölaynu | מִמָּרוֹם יְלַמְּדוּ עָלָיו וְעָלֵינוּ |
| z'chus shet'hay l'mishmeres | זְכוּת שֶׁתְּהֵא לְמִשְׁמֶרֶת |
| shölom, v'nisö v'röchöh may-ays | שָׁלוֹם, וְנִשָּׂא בְרָכָה מֵאֵת |
| adonöy utz'dököh may-elohay | יְהֹוָה וּצְדָקָה מֵאֱלֹהֵי |
| yish-aynu, v'nimtzö chayn v'saychel | יִשְׁעֵנוּ, וְנִמְצָא חֵן וְשֵׂכֶל |
| tov b'aynay elohim v'ödöm. | טוֹב בְּעֵינֵי אֱלֹהִים וְאָדָם: |

From heaven, may there be invoked upon him and upon us such merit which will bring enduring peace. May we receive blessing from the Lord and kindness from God our Deliverer, and may we find grace and good understanding in the eyes of God and man.

103

On Shabbat add: **בשבת:**

Hörachamön hu yan-chi-laynu הָרַחֲמָן הוּא יַנְחִילֵנוּ
l'yom shekulo shabös um'nuchöh לְיוֹם שֶׁכֻּלּוֹ שַׁבָּת וּמְנוּחָה
l'cha-yay hö-olömim. לְחַיֵּי הָעוֹלָמִים:

*May the Merciful One let us inherit that day which will be all Shabbat and rest for life everlasting.*

Horachamön hu yan-chi-laynu הָרַחֲמָן הוּא יַנְחִילֵנוּ
l'yom shekulo tov. לְיוֹם שֶׁכֻּלּוֹ טוֹב:

*May the Merciful One let us inherit that day which is all good.*

Hörachamön hu y'zakaynu li-mos הָרַחֲמָן הוּא יְזַכֵּנוּ לִימוֹת
hamöshi-ach ul'cha-yay hö-olöm הַמָּשִׁיחַ וּלְחַיֵּי הָעוֹלָם
ha-bö. Migdol y'shu-os malko v'o-seh הַבָּא. מִגְדּוֹל יְשׁוּעוֹת מַלְכּוֹ וְעֹשֶׂה
chesed lim'shicho l'dövid ul'zar-o חֶסֶד לִמְשִׁיחוֹ לְדָוִד וּלְזַרְעוֹ
ad olöm. O-seh shölom bim'romöv עַד עוֹלָם: עֹשֶׂה שָׁלוֹם בִּמְרוֹמָיו
hu ya-aseh shölom ölaynu v'al הוּא יַעֲשֶׂה שָׁלוֹם עָלֵינוּ וְעַל
köl yisrö-ayl v'im'ru ömayn. כָּל יִשְׂרָאֵל וְאִמְרוּ אָמֵן:

*May the Merciful One grant us the privilege of reaching the days of the Mashiach and the life of the World to Come. He is a tower of deliverance to His king, and bestows kindness upon His anointed, to David and his descendants forever. He Who makes peace in His heavens, may He make peace for us and for all Israel; and say, Amen.*

Y'ru es adonöy k'doshöv ki ayn
machsor liray-öv. K'firim röshu
v'rö-ayvu v'dor'shay adonöy lo
yach-s'ru chöl tov. Hodu la-donöy
ki tov ki l'olöm chasdo.
Posay-ach es yödechö umasbi-a
l'chöl chai rö-tzon. Böruch ha-gever
asher yivtach ba-donöy v'hö-yöh
adonöy miv-tacho.

יְראוּ אֶת יְהֹוָה קְדשָׁיו כִּי אֵין
מַחְסוֹר לִירֵאָיו : כְּפִירִים רָשׁוּ
וְרָעֵבוּ וְדֹרְשֵׁי יְהֹוָה לֹא
יַחְסְרוּ כָל טוֹב : הוֹדוּ לַיָי
כִּי טוֹב כִּי לְעוֹלָם חַסְדּוֹ :
פּוֹתֵחַ אֶת יָדֶךָ וּמַשְׂבִּיעַ
לְכָל חַי רָצוֹן : בָּרוּךְ הַגֶּבֶר
אֲשֶׁר יִבְטַח בַּיָי וְהָיָה
יְהֹוָה מִבְטַחוֹ :

*Fear the Lord, you His holy ones, for those who fear Him suffer no want. Young lions are in need and go hungry, but those who seek the Lord shall not lack any good. Give thanks to the Lord for He is good, for His kindness is everlasting. You open Your hand and satisfy the desire of every living thing. Blessed is the man who trusts in the Lord, and the Lord will be his security.*

Lift the cup with your right hand. Transfer it to the left hand. Lower it into the cupped palm of your right hand (if you write with your left hand, reverse). Lift the cup at least 3 inches above the table. Recite the following blessing:

Böruch atöh adonöy, elohaynu
melech hö-olöm, boray p'ri ha-göfen.

בָּרוּךְ אַתָּה יְיָ, אֱלֹהֵינוּ
מֶלֶךְ הָעוֹלָם, בּוֹרֵא פְּרִי הַגָּפֶן :

*Blessed are You, Lord our God, King of the universe, Who creates the fruit of the vine.*

**Drink the third cup of wine (at least two ounces), while reclining to the left.**

# *The Cup of Elijah*

It is customary at this point in the seder to open the door leading into the home in the hope that Elijah will come, signaling the arrival of *Moshiach* (the messiah), ushering in the era of world peace and perfection. This meaningful custom expresses and fortifies our faith, and that of our children, in his imminent arrival.

The fourth cup of wine is filled. It is customary to rise from the seder table and stand by the door leading to the street while reciting the following passage. When Pesach takes place on a weekday, a lighted candle is taken in hand. This moment is also a propitious time to pray for one's spiritual and physical needs.

שְׁפֹוךְ חֲמָתְךָ אֶל הַגּוֹיִם
אֲשֶׁר לֹא יְדָעוּךָ, וְעַל מַמְלָכוֹת
אֲשֶׁר בְּשִׁמְךָ לֹא קָרָאוּ: כִּי אָכַל
אֶת יַעֲקֹב וְאֶת נָוֵהוּ הֵשַׁמּוּ:
שְׁפָךְ עֲלֵיהֶם זַעְמֶךָ וַחֲרוֹן
אַפְּךָ יַשִּׂיגֵם: תִּרְדּוֹף בְּאַף
וְתַשְׁמִידֵם מִתַּחַת
שְׁמֵי יְהֹוָה:

Sh'foch chamös'chö el ha-gö-yim asher lo y'dö-uchö, v'al mam-löchos asher b'shim'chö lo köröu. Ki öchal es ya-akov v'es növay-hu hay-shamu. Sh'föch alay-hem za-mechö va-charon ap'chö yasi-gaym. Tirdof b'af v'sash-midaym mitachas sh'may adonöy.

*Pour out Your wrath upon the nations that do not acknowledge You, and upon the kingdoms that do not call upon Your Name, for they have devoured Yaakov and* destroyed his habitation. *Pour out Your anger against them, and let the wrath of Your fury overtake them. Pursue them with anger and destroy them from beneath the heavens of the Lord.*

---

## • *Hallel - Nirtzoh* •
## Verses of Praise - Acceptance

---

We are nearing the conclusion of the seder. At this point, having recognized the Almighty and His unique guidance of His people Israel, we go still further and turn to sing His praises. After reciting the hallel, we recite the blessing for wine and drink the fourth and final cup of wine.

| | |
|---|---|
| Lo lönu adonöy, lo lönu, | לֹא לָנוּ יְהֹוָה, לֹא לָנוּ, |
| ki l'shim'chöh tayn kövod, al | כִּי לְשִׁמְךָ תֵּן כָּבוֹד, עַל |
| chas-d'chö al amitechöh. Lömöh | חַסְדְּךָ עַל אֲמִתֶּךָ: לָמָּה |
| yom'ru ha-gö-yim, ayay nö | יֹאמְרוּ הַגּוֹיִם, אַיֵּה נָא |
| elohay-hem. Vay-lohaynu | אֱלֹהֵיהֶם: וֵאלֹהֵינוּ |
| va-shömö-yim, kol asher chöfaytz | בַשָּׁמָיִם, כֹּל אֲשֶׁר חָפֵץ |
| ösöh. Atza-bay-hem kesef v'zöhöv, | עָשָׂה: עֲצַבֵּיהֶם כֶּסֶף וְזָהָב, |
| ma-asay y'day ödöm. Peh löhem v'lo | מַעֲשֵׂי יְדֵי אָדָם: פֶּה לָהֶם וְלֹא |
| y'dabay-ru, ayna-yim löhem v'lo yir-u. | יְדַבֵּרוּ, עֵינַיִם לָהֶם וְלֹא יִרְאוּ: |
| Özna-yim löhem v'lo yishmö-u, | אָזְנַיִם לָהֶם וְלֹא יִשְׁמָעוּ, |
| af löhem v'lo y'richun. Y'day-hem | אַף לָהֶם וְלֹא יְרִיחוּן: יְדֵיהֶם |

107

v'lo y'mishun, rag-layhem v'lo וְלֹא יְמִישׁוּן, רַגְלֵיהֶם וְלֹא
y'halaychu, lo yeh-gu big'ronöm. יְהַלֵּכוּ, לֹא יֶהְגּוּ בִּגְרוֹנָם :
K'mohem yih-yu osay-hem, kol asher כְּמוֹהֶם יִהְיוּ עֹשֵׂיהֶם, כֹּל אֲשֶׁר
botay-ach bö-hem. Yisrö-ayl b'tach בֹּטֵחַ בָּהֶם : יִשְׂרָאֵל בְּטַח
ba-donöy, ezröm umöginöm hu. בַּיהוָה, עֶזְרָם וּמָגִנָּם הוּא :
Bays aharon bit'chu va-donöy, ezröm בֵּית אַהֲרֹן בִּטְחוּ בַיהוָה, עֶזְרָם
umöginöm hu. Yir'ay adonöy bit'chu וּמָגִנָּם הוּא : יִרְאֵי יְהוָה בִּטְחוּ
va-donöy, ezröm umö-ginöm hu. בַיהוָה, עֶזְרָם וּמָגִנָּם הוּא :

*Not for our sake, Lord, not for our sake, but for Your Name's sake give glory for the sake of Your kindness and for Your truth. Why should the nations say, "Where now is their God?" Our God is in heaven, whatever He desires He does. Their idols are silver and gold, the work of human hands. They have a mouth, but cannot speak; they have eyes, but cannot see. They have ears, but cannot hear; they have a nose, but cannot smell. Their hands cannot feel; their feet cannot walk; they can make no sounds with their throats. Like them shall be their makers, everyone that trusts in them. Israel trust in the Lord, their help and their shield is He. House of Aharon trust in the Lord, He is their help and their shield. You who fear the Lord, trust in the Lord; He is their help and their shield.*

Adonöy z'chöronu y'vöraych, יְהוָה זְכָרָנוּ יְבָרֵךְ,
y'vöraych es bays yisrö-ayl, y'vöraych יְבָרֵךְ אֶת בֵּית יִשְׂרָאֵל, יְבָרֵךְ
es bays aharon. Y'vöraych yi'ray אֶת בֵּית אַהֲרֹן : יְבָרֵךְ יִרְאֵי
adonöy, ha-k'tanim im ha-g'dolim. יְהוָה, הַקְּטַנִּים עִם הַגְּדֹלִים :
Yosayf adonöy alaychem, alaychem יֹסֵף יְהוָה עֲלֵיכֶם, עֲלֵיכֶם
v'al b'naychem. B'ruchim atem וְעַל בְּנֵיכֶם : בְּרוּכִים אַתֶּם

ladonöy osay shöma-yim vö-öretz.   לַיהוָה, עֹשֵׂה שָׁמַיִם וָאָרֶץ׃
Ha-shöma-yim, shöma-yim ladonöy,   הַשָּׁמַיִם, שָׁמַיִם לַיהוָה,
v'hö-öretz nösan liv'nay ö-döm.   וְהָאָרֶץ נָתַן לִבְנֵי אָדָם׃
Lo ha-maysim y'ha-l'lu yöh, v'lo   לֹא הַמֵּתִים יְהַלְלוּ יָהּ, וְלֹא
köl yor'day dumöh. Va-anachnu   כָּל יֹרְדֵי דוּמָה׃ וַאֲנַחְנוּ
n'vö-raych yöh, may-atöh v'ad   נְבָרֵךְ יָהּ, מֵעַתָּה וְעַד
olöm, ha-l'luyöh.   עוֹלָם, הַלְלוּיָהּ׃

*The Lord, Who is ever-mindful of us, will bless, He will bless the House of Israel, He will bless the House of Aharon. He will bless those who fear the Lord, the small with the great. May the Lord increase [His blessings on] you, to you and to your children. You are blessed to the Lord, Maker of heaven and earth. The heaven is the heaven of the Lord, but the earth He gave to the children of man. The dead do not praise the Lord, nor do those who descend to silence. But we will bless God, from now and forever. Praise the Lord.*

Öhavti ki yishma adonöy es koli   אָהַבְתִּי כִּי יִשְׁמַע יְהוָה אֶת קוֹלִי
ta-cha-nunöy. Ki hi-töh öz'noy li,   תַּחֲנוּנָי׃ כִּי הִטָּה אָזְנוֹ לִי,
uv'yömai ekrö. Aföfuni chev'lay   וּבְיָמַי אֶקְרָא׃ אֲפָפוּנִי חֶבְלֵי
möves um'tzöray sh'ol m'tzö-uni,   מָוֶת וּמְצָרֵי שְׁאוֹל מְצָאוּנִי,
tzöröh v'yögon emtzö. Uv'shaym   צָרָה וְיָגוֹן אֶמְצָא׃ וּבְשֵׁם
adonöy ekrö, önöh adonöy   יְהוָה אֶקְרָא, אָנָּה יְהוָה
mal'töh nafshi. Chanun adonöy   מַלְּטָה נַפְשִׁי׃ חַנּוּן יְהוָה
v'tzadik, vaylo-haynu m'rachaym.   וְצַדִּיק, וֵאלֹהֵינוּ מְרַחֵם׃
Shomayr p'sö-yim adonöy, dalosi   שֹׁמֵר פְּתָאִים יְהוָה, דַּלּוֹתִי

**109**

v'li y'hoshi-a. Shuvi nafshi
llim'nuchöy-chi, ki adonöy gömal
ölöy-chi. Ki chi-latztö nafshi
mimö-ves es ayni min dim-öh
es ragli midechi. Eshalaych lif'nay
adonöy, b'ar'tzos ha-cha-yim.
He-emanti ki adabayr, ani önisi
m'od. Ani ömarti v'chöf'zi, köl
hö-ödom kozayv.

וְלִי יְהוֹשִׁיעַ : שׁוּבִי נַפְשִׁי
לִמְנוּחָיְכִי, כִּי יְהוָה גָּמַל
עָלָיְכִי : כִּי חִלַּצְתָּ נַפְשִׁי
מִמָּוֶת אֶת עֵינִי מִן דִּמְעָה
אֶת רַגְלִי מִדֶּחִי : אֶתְהַלֵּךְ לִפְנֵי
יְהוָה, בְּאַרְצוֹת הַחַיִּים :
הֶאֱמַנְתִּי כִּי אֲדַבֵּר, אֲנִי עָנִיתִי
מְאֹד : אֲנִי אָמַרְתִּי בְחָפְזִי,
כָּל הָאָדָם כֹּזֵב :

*I would love if the Lord would listen to my voice, to my supplications. If He would
turn His ear to me on the days that I call. I am encompassed with the pangs of
death; the misery of the grave came upon me; I encounter trouble and sorrow. And
upon the Name of the Lord I called, "Lord, I implore you, deliver my soul!"
Gracious is the Lord and righteous; and our God is merciful. The Lord guards the
simpletons; I was brought low, but He saved me. Return, my soul, to your rest, for
the Lord has dealt kindly with you. For You have delivered my soul from death,
my eyes from tears, my feet from stumbling. I will walk before the Lord in the
world of the living. I had faith even when I said: "I suffer so greatly," [even when] I
said in my haste, "All men are deceitful."*

Möh öshiv ladonöy köl tag-mulohi
ölöy. Kos y'shu-os esöh, uv'shaym
adonöy ekrö. N'dörai ladonöy
asha-laym neg-döh nö l'chöl amo.
Yökör b'ay-nay adonöy, ha-möv-söh

מָה אָשִׁיב לַיהוָה, כָּל תַּגְמוּלוֹהִי
עָלָי : כּוֹס יְשׁוּעוֹת אֶשָּׂא, וּבְשֵׁם
יְהוָה אֶקְרָא : נְדָרַי לַיהוָה
אֲשַׁלֵּם, נֶגְדָה נָא לְכָל עַמּוֹ :
יָקָר בְּעֵינֵי יְהוָה, הַמָּוְתָה

la-chasidöv. Önö adonöy ki ani
av'dechö, ani av-d'chö ben amösechö,
pitach-tö l'mosay-röy. L'chö ezbach
zevach todöh, uv'shaym adonöy
ekrö. N'dörai ladonöy asha-laym,
neg-döh nöh l'chöl amo. B'chatz'ros
bays adonöy, b'sochay-chi
y'ru-shölö-yim, ha-l'lu-yöh.

לַחֲסִידָיו : אָנָּה יְהוָֹה כִּי אֲנִי
עַבְדֶּךָ, אֲנִי עַבְדְּךָ בֶּן אֲמָתֶךָ,
פִּתַּחְתָּ לְמוֹסֵרָי : לְךָ אֶזְבַּח
זֶבַח תּוֹדָה, וּבְשֵׁם יְהוָֹה
אֶקְרָא : נְדָרַי לַיהוָֹה אֲשַׁלֵּם,
נֶגְדָה נָּא לְכָל עַמּוֹ : בְּחַצְרוֹת
בֵּית יְהוָֹה, בְּתוֹכֵכִי
יְרוּשָׁלָיִם, הַלְלוּיָהּ :

*What can I tender to the Lord for all His kindness to me? I will lift up the cup of
salvations and call upon the Name of the Lord. I will pay my vows to the Lord,
now, in the presence of all His people. Grievous in the eyes of the Lord is the death
of His pious ones. I thank You, Lord, for I am Your servant; I am Your servant, the
son of Your maidservant; You have loosened my bonds. To you I will offer a
thanksgiving sacrifice, and upon the Name of the Lord I will call. I will pay my
vows to the Lord, now, in the presence of all His people. In the courtyards of the
House of the Lord, in your midst, Jerusalem. Praise the Lord.*

Ha-l'lu es adonöy köl gö-yim,
shab'chuhu köl hö-umim. Ki növar
ölaynu chasdo ve-emes adonöy
l'olöm, ha-l'lu-yöh.

הַלְלוּ אֶת יְהוָֹה כָּל גּוֹיִם,
שַׁבְּחוּהוּ כָּל הָאֻמִּים : כִּי גָבַר
עָלֵינוּ חַסְדּוֹ וֶאֱמֶת יְהוָֹה
לְעוֹלָם, הַלְלוּיָהּ :

*Praise the Lord all you nations; extol Him, all you peoples. For His kindness was
mighty over us, and the truth of the Lord is everlasting. Praise the Lord.*

Hodu ladonöy ki tov,     הוֹדוּ לַיהוָה כִּי טוֹב,
ki l'olöm chasdo.     כִּי לְעוֹלָם חַסְדּוֹ:
Yomar nöh yisrö-ayl,     יֹאמַר נָא יִשְׂרָאֵל,
ki l'olöm chasdo.     כִּי לְעוֹלָם חַסְדּוֹ:
Yom'ru nö bays aharon,     יֹאמְרוּ נָא בֵית אַהֲרֹן,
ki l'olöm chasdo.     כִּי לְעוֹלָם חַסְדּוֹ:
Yom'ru nö yir'ay adonöy,     יֹאמְרוּ נָא יִרְאֵי יְהוָה,
ki l'olöm chasdo.     כִּי לְעוֹלָם חַסְדּוֹ:

*Offer praise to the Lord for He is good, for His kindness is everlasting. Let Israel declare that His kindness is everlasting. Let the house of Aaron declare that His kindness is everlasting. Let all those who fear the Lord declare that His kindness is everlasting.*

Min ha-maytzer körösi yöh, önöni     מִן הַמֵּצַר קָרָאתִי יָּהּ, עֲנָנִי
va-mer-chav yöh. Adonöy li lo irö,     בַמֶּרְחָב יָהּ: יְהוָה לִי לֹא אִירָא,
mah ya-aseh li ödöm. Adonöy     מַה יַּעֲשֶׂה לִי אָדָם: יְהוָה
li b'oz'roy, va-ani er-eh v'son'öy.     לִי בְּעֹזְרָי, וַאֲנִי אֶרְאֶה בְשֹׂנְאָי:
Tov la-chasos badonöy, mib'to-ach     טוֹב לַחֲסוֹת בַּיהוָה, מִבְּטֹחַ
bö-ödöm. Tov la-chasos badonöy,     בָּאָדָם: טוֹב לַחֲסוֹת בַּיהוָה,
mib'to-ach bin'divim. Köl go-yim     מִבְּטֹחַ בִּנְדִיבִים: כָּל גּוֹיִם
s'vövuni, b'shaym adonöy ki amilam.     סְבָבוּנִי, בְּשֵׁם יְהוָה כִּי אֲמִילַם:
Sabuni gam s'vövuni, b'shaym     סַבּוּנִי גַם סְבָבוּנִי, בְּשֵׁם
adonöy ki amilam. Sabuni chid'vorim     יְהוָה כִּי אֲמִילַם: סַבּוּנִי כִדְבֹרִים
do-achu k'aysh ko-tzim, b'shaym     דֹּעֲכוּ כְּאֵשׁ קוֹצִים, בְּשֵׁם
adonöy ki amilam. Döcho d'chisani     יְהוָה כִּי אֲמִילַם: דָּחֹה דְחִיתַנִי

linpol, vadonöy azöröni. Özi v'zimrös yöh, va-y'hi li lishu-öh. Kol rinöh vishu-öh b'öhölay tzadikim, y'min adonöy osöh chö-yil. Y'min adonöy romaymöh, y'min adonöy osöh chö-yil. Lo ömus ki ech-yeh, va-asapayr ma-asay yöh. Yasor yis'rani yöh, v'lamöves lo n'sönöni. Pis'chu li sha-aray tzedek, övö vöm od-eh yöh. Zeh ha-sha-ar ladonöy, tzadikim yövo-u vo. Od'chö ki anisöni, vat'hi li lishu-ö. Od'chö ki anisöni, vat'hi li lishu-ö. E-ven mö-asu ha-bonim, hö-y'söh l'rosh pinöh. E-ven mö-asu ha-bonim, hö-y'söh 'rosh pinöh. May-ays adonöy hö-y'söh zos, hi niflös b'aynaynu. May-ays adonöy hö-y'söh zos, hi niflös b'aynaynu. Zeh ha-yom ösö adonöy, nögilöh v'nism'chöh vo. Zeh ha-yom ösö adonöy, nögilöh v'nism'chöh vo.

לִנְפֹּל, וַיהוָֹה עֲזָרָנִי : עָזִּי וְזִמְרָת יָהּ, וַיְהִי לִי לִישׁוּעָה : קוֹל רִנָּה וִישׁוּעָה בְּאָהֳלֵי צַדִּיקִים, יְמִין יְהוָֹה עֹשָׂה חָיִל : יְמִין יְהוָֹה רוֹמֵמָה, יְמִין יְהוָֹה עֹשָׂה חָיִל : לֹא אָמוּת כִּי אֶחְיֶה, וַאֲסַפֵּר מַעֲשֵׂי יָהּ : יַסֹּר יִסְּרַנִּי יָהּ, וְלַמָּוֶת לֹא נְתָנָנִי : פִּתְחוּ לִי שַׁעֲרֵי צֶדֶק, אָבֹא בָם אוֹדֶה יָהּ : זֶה הַשַּׁעַר לַיהוָֹה, צַדִּיקִים יָבֹאוּ בוֹ : אוֹדְךָ כִּי עֲנִיתָנִי, וַתְּהִי לִי לִישׁוּעָה : אוֹדְךָ כִּי עֲנִיתָנִי, וַתְּהִי לִי לִישׁוּעָה : אֶבֶן מָאֲסוּ הַבּוֹנִים, הָיְתָה לְרֹאשׁ פִּנָּה : אֶבֶן מָאֲסוּ הַבּוֹנִים, הָיְתָה לְרֹאשׁ פִּנָּה : מֵאֵת יְהוָֹה הָיְתָה זֹּאת, הִיא נִפְלָאת בְּעֵינֵינוּ : מֵאֵת יְהוָֹה הָיְתָה זֹּאת, הִיא נִפְלָאת בְּעֵינֵינוּ : זֶה הַיּוֹם עָשָׂה יְהוָֹה, נָגִילָה וְנִשְׂמְחָה בוֹ : זֶה הַיּוֹם עָשָׂה יְהוָֹה, נָגִילָה וְנִשְׂמְחָה בוֹ :

*From out of distress I called to God; with abounding relief, God answered me. The Lord is with me, I do not fear – what can man do to me? The Lord is with me*

113

*through my helpers, I will see [the downfall of] my enemies. It is better to rely on the Lord than to trust in man. It is better to take refuge in the Lord than to trust in nobles. All nations surround me; in the Name of the Lord I cut them down. They encircle me and surround me; in the Name of the Lord I cut them down. They encircle me like bees; they are extinguished like flaming thorns; in the Name of the Lord I cut them down. You [my foes] pushed me again and again to fall, but the Lord helped me. God is my strength and song, and this has been my salvation. The sound of rejoicing and salvation is in the tents of the righteous: "The right hand of the Lord performs deeds of valor. The right hand of the Lord is exalted; the right hand of the Lord performs deeds of valor!" I shall not die, for I shall live and relate the deeds of God. God chastised me repeatedly, but He did not hand me over to death. Open for me the gates of righteousness; I will enter and thank God. This is the gate of the Lord; the righteous shall enter it. I thank You for You answered me, and You have become my salvation.* (Repeat this verse) *The stone which the builders despised has become the cornerstone.* (Repeat this verse) *This is from the Lord; it is wondrous in our eyes.* (Repeat this verse) *This is the day the Lord has made, let us be glad and rejoice on it.* (Repeat this verse)

| | |
|---|---|
| Önö adonöy hoshi-öh nö. | אָנָּא יְהֹוָה הוֹשִׁיעָה נָּא : |
| Önö adonöy hoshi-öh nö. | אָנָּא יְהֹוָה הוֹשִׁיעָה נָּא : |
| Önö adonöy hatz-lichöh nö. | אָנָּא יְהֹוָה הַצְלִיחָה נָּא : |
| Önö adonöy hatz-lichöh nö. | אָנָּא יְהֹוָה הַצְלִיחָה נָּא : |

*We implore You, Lord, deliver us. We implore You, Lord, deliver us. We implore You, Lord, grant us success. We implore You, Lord, grant us success.*

| | |
|---|---|
| Böruch ha-böh b'shaym adonöy, | בָּרוּךְ הַבָּא בְּשֵׁם יְהֹוָה, |
| bayrach-nuchem mibays adonöy. | בֵּרַכְנוּכֶם מִבֵּית יְהֹוָה : |
| Böruch ha-böh b'shaym adonöy, | בָּרוּךְ הַבָּא בְּשֵׁם יְהֹוָה, |
| bayrach-nuchem mibays adonöy. | בֵּרַכְנוּכֶם מִבֵּית יְהֹוָה : |
| Ayl adonöy va-yöeyr lönu, is'ru chag | אֵל יְהֹוָה וַיָּאֶר לָנוּ, אִסְרוּ חַג |
| ba-avosim, ad kar'nos ha-mizbay-ach. | בַּעֲבֹתִים, עַד קַרְנוֹת הַמִּזְבֵּחַ : |
| Ayl adonöy va-yöeyr lönu, is'ru | אֵל יְהֹוָה וַיָּאֶר לָנוּ, אִסְרוּ |
| chag ba-avosim, ad kar'nos | חַג בַּעֲבֹתִים, עַד קַרְנוֹת |
| ha-mizbay-ach. Ayli atöh v'odekö, | הַמִּזְבֵּחַ : אֵלִי אַתָּה וְאוֹדֶךָּ, |
| elohai aro-m'mekö. Ayli atöh v'odekö, | אֱלֹהַי אֲרוֹמְמֶךָ : אֵלִי אַתָּה וְאוֹדֶךָּ, |
| elohai aro-m'mekö. Hodu ladonöy | אֱלֹהַי אֲרוֹמְמֶךָ : הוֹדוּ לַיהֹוָה |
| ki tov, ki l'olöm chasdo. Hodu | כִּי טוֹב, כִּי לְעוֹלָם חַסְדּוֹ : הוֹדוּ |
| ladonöy ki tov, ki l'olöm chasdo. | לַיהֹוָה כִּי טוֹב, כִּי לְעוֹלָם חַסְדּוֹ : |

*Blessed is he who comes in the Name of the Lord; we bless you from the House of the Lord.* (Repeat this verse) *The Lord is a benevolent God and He has given us light; bind the festival offering with cords until [you bring it to] the corners of the altar.* (Repeat this verse) *You are my God and I will praise You, my God – and I will exalt You.* (Repeat this verse) *Praise the Lord for He is good, for His kindness is everlasting.* (Repeat this verse)

| | |
|---|---|
| Y'hal'luchö adonö elohaynu köl | יְהַלְלוּךָ יְהֹוָה אֱלֹהֵינוּ כָּל |
| ma-asechö, va-chasidechö tzadikim | מַעֲשֶׂיךָ, וַחֲסִידֶיךָ צַדִּיקִים |
| osay r'tzonechö, v'chöl am'chö bays | עוֹשֵׂי רְצוֹנֶךָ, וְכָל עַמְּךָ בֵּית |
| yisrö-ayl, b'rinöh yodu vivö-r'chu, | יִשְׂרָאֵל, בְּרִנָּה יוֹדוּ וִיבָרְכוּ, |
| vishab'chu vifö-aru, viro-m'mu | וִישַׁבְּחוּ וִיפָאֲרוּ, וִירוֹמְמוּ |

v'ya-ari-tzu, v'yakdishu v'yamlichu
es shim'chö malkaynu. Ki l'chö
tov l'hodos, ul'shim'chö nö-eh
l'zamayr, ki may-olöm v'ad
olöm atöh ayl.

וְיַעֲרִיצוּ, וְיַקְדִּישׁוּ וְיַמְלִיכוּ
אֶת שִׁמְךָ מַלְכֵּנוּ. כִּי לְךָ
טוֹב לְהוֹדוֹת, וּלְשִׁמְךָ נָאֶה
לְזַמֵּר, כִּי מֵעוֹלָם וְעַד
עוֹלָם אַתָּה אֵל.

*Lord our God, all Your works will praise You, and Your pious ones, the righteous
who do Your will, and all Your people, the House of Israel, with joyous song will
thank, bless, praise, glorify, exalt, extol, sanctify, and proclaim the sovereignty of
Your Name, our King. For to you it is good to give thanks, and to Your Name it is
pleasant to sing praise, for from [the highest] world to [the lowest] world You are
Almighty.*

Hodu ladonöy ki tov,
הוֹדוּ לַיהוָֹה כִּי טוֹב,

ki l'olöm chasdo.
כִּי לְעוֹלָם חַסְדּוֹ:

Hodu lay-lohay hö-elohim,
הוֹדוּ לֵאלֹהֵי הָאֱלֹהִים,

ki l'olöm chasdo.
כִּי לְעוֹלָם חַסְדּוֹ:

Hodu la-adonay hö-adonim,
הוֹדוּ לַאֲדֹנֵי הָאֲדֹנִים,

ki l'olöm chasdo.
כִּי לְעוֹלָם חַסְדּוֹ:

L'osay niflö-os g'dolos
לְעֹשֵׂה נִפְלָאוֹת גְּדֹלוֹת

l'vado, ki l'olöm chasdo.
לְבַדּוֹ, כִּי לְעוֹלָם חַסְדּוֹ:

L'osay ha-shöma-yim bi-s'vunöh,
לְעֹשֵׂה הַשָּׁמַיִם בִּתְבוּנָה,

ki l'olöm chasdo.
כִּי לְעוֹלָם חַסְדּוֹ:

L'roka hö-öretz al ha-mö-yim,
לְרוֹקַע הָאָרֶץ עַל הַמָּיִם,

ki l'olöm chasdo.
כִּי לְעוֹלָם חַסְדּוֹ:

L'osay orim g'dolim,
לְעֹשֵׂה אוֹרִים גְּדֹלִים,

| | |
|---|---|
| ki l'olöm chasdo. | כִּי לְעוֹלָם חַסְדּוֹ : |
| Es ha-shemesh l'mem-sheles | אֶת הַשֶּׁמֶשׁ לְמֶמְשֶׁלֶת |
| ba-yom, ki l'olöm chasdo. | בַּיּוֹם, כִּי לְעוֹלָם חַסְדּוֹ : |
| Es ha-yöray-ach v'cho-chövim | אֶת הַיָּרֵחַ וְכוֹכָבִים |
| l'memsh'los ba-löy-lö, | לְמֶמְשְׁלוֹת בַּלָּיְלָה, |
| ki l'olöm chasdo. | כִּי לְעוֹלָם חַסְדּוֹ : |
| L'makay mitzra-yim biv'choray-hem, | לְמַכֵּה מִצְרַיִם בִּבְכוֹרֵיהֶם, |
| ki l'olöm chasdo. | כִּי לְעוֹלָם חַסְדּוֹ : |
| Va-yo-tzay yisrö-ayl mitochöm, | וַיּוֹצֵא יִשְׂרָאֵל מִתּוֹכָם, |
| ki l'olöm chasdo. | כִּי לְעוֹלָם חַסְדּוֹ : |
| B'yöd chazököh uviz'ro-ah n'tu-yöh, | בְּיָד חֲזָקָה וּבִזְרוֹעַ נְטוּיָה, |
| ki l'olöm chasdo. | כִּי לְעוֹלָם חַסְדּוֹ : |
| L'gozayr yam suf lig'zörim, | לְגֹזֵר יַם סוּף לִגְזָרִים, |
| ki l'olöm chasdo. | כִּי לְעוֹלָם חַסְדּוֹ : |
| V'he-evir yisrö-ayl b'socho, | וְהֶעֱבִיר יִשְׂרָאֵל בְּתוֹכוֹ, |
| ki l'olöm chasdo. | כִּי לְעוֹלָם חַסְדּוֹ : |
| V'ni-ayr par-oh v'chaylo v'yam suf, | וְנִעֵר פַּרְעֹה וְחֵילוֹ בְיַם סוּף, |
| ki l'olöm chasdo. | כִּי לְעוֹלָם חַסְדּוֹ : |
| L'molich amo bamidbör, | לְמוֹלִיךְ עַמּוֹ בַּמִּדְבָּר, |
| ki l'olöm chasdo. | כִּי לְעוֹלָם חַסְדּוֹ : |
| L'makay m'löchim g'dolim, | לְמַכֵּה מְלָכִים גְּדֹלִים, |
| ki l'olöm chasdo. | כִּי לְעוֹלָם חַסְדּוֹ : |
| Va-yaharog m'löchim adirim, | וַיַּהֲרֹג מְלָכִים אַדִּירִים, |
| ki l'olöm chasdo. | כִּי לְעוֹלָם חַסְדּוֹ : |

| | |
|---|---|
| L'sichon melech hö-emori, | לְסִיחוֹן מֶלֶךְ הָאֱמֹרִי, |
| ki l'olöm chasdo. | כִּי לְעוֹלָם חַסְדּוֹ: |
| U-l'og melech ha-böshön, | וּלְעוֹג מֶלֶךְ הַבָּשָׁן, |
| ki l'olöm chasdo. | כִּי לְעוֹלָם חַסְדּוֹ: |
| V'nösan ar-tzöm l'na-chalöh, | וְנָתַן אַרְצָם לְנַחֲלָה, |
| ki l'olöm chasdo. | כִּי לְעוֹלָם חַסְדּוֹ: |
| Na-chalöh l'yisrö-ayl avdo, | נַחֲלָה לְיִשְׂרָאֵל עַבְדּוֹ, |
| ki l'olöm chasdo. | כִּי לְעוֹלָם חַסְדּוֹ: |
| Sheb'shiflaynu zöchar lönu, | שֶׁבְּשִׁפְלֵנוּ זָכַר לָנוּ, |
| ki l'olöm chasdo. | כִּי לְעוֹלָם חַסְדּוֹ: |
| Va-yif-r'kaynu mitzöraynu, | וַיִּפְרְקֵנוּ מִצָּרֵינוּ, |
| ki l'olöm chasdo. | כִּי לְעוֹלָם חַסְדּוֹ: |
| Nosayn lechem l'chöl bösör, | נֹתֵן לֶחֶם לְכָל בָּשָׂר, |
| ki l'olöm chasdo. | כִּי לְעוֹלָם חַסְדּוֹ: |
| Hodu l'ayl ha-shömö-yim, | הוֹדוּ לְאֵל הַשָּׁמָיִם, |
| ki l'olöm chasdo. | כִּי לְעוֹלָם חַסְדּוֹ: |

*Praise the Lord for He is good, for His kindness is everlasting; Praise the God of the supernal beings, for His kindness is everlasting; Praise the Master of the heavenly hosts, for His kindness is everlasting; Who alone performs great wonders, for His kindness is everlasting; Who makes the heavens with understanding, for His kindness is everlasting; Who spreads forth the earth above the waters, for His kindness is everlasting; Who makes the great lights, for His kindness is everlasting; The sun to rule by day, for His kindness is everlasting; The moon and stars to rule by night, for His kindness is everlasting; Who struck Egypt through its first-born, for His kindness is everlasting; And brought Israel out of their midst, for His kindness is everlasting; With a strong hand and with an outstretched arm, for His kindness is everlasting; Who split the Sea of Reeds into sections, for His kindness is everlasting; And brought Israel across it, for His kindness is everlasting; And cast Pharaoh and his army into the Sea of Reeds, for His kindness is everlasting; Who led His people through the desert, for His kindness is everlasting; Who struck down great kings, for His kindness is everlasting; And slew mighty kings, for His kindness is everlasting; Sichon, king of the Amorites, for His kindness is everlasting; And Og, king of Bashan, for His kindness is everlasting; And gave their land as a heritage, for His kindness is everlasting; A heritage to Israel His servant, for His kindness is everlasting; Who remembered us in our humiliation, for His kindness is everlasting; And redeemed us from our oppressors, for His kindness is everlasting; Who gives food to all flesh, for His kindness is everlasting; Praise the God of heaven, for His kindness is everlasting.*

| | |
|---|---|
| Nish'mas köl chai t'vöraych | נִשְׁמַת כָּל חַי תְּבָרֵךְ |
| es shim'chö adonöy elohaynu. | אֶת שִׁמְךָ יְהֹוָה אֱלֹהֵינוּ. |
| V'ru-ach köl bösör t'föayr us'romaym | וְרוּחַ כָּל בָּשָׂר תְּפָאֵר וּתְרוֹמֵם |
| zich-r'chö malkaynu tömid, min | זִכְרְךָ מַלְכֵּנוּ תָּמִיד, מִן |
| hö-olöm v'ad hö-olöm atöh ayl. | הָעוֹלָם וְעַד הָעוֹלָם אַתָּה אֵל, |
| umibal-ödechö ayn lönu melech | וּמִבַּלְעָדֶיךָ אֵין לָנוּ מֶלֶךְ |
| go-ayl umoshi-a, po-deh umatzil | גּוֹאֵל וּמוֹשִׁיעַ, פּוֹדֶה וּמַצִּיל |
| um'farnays v'o-neh um'rachaym | וּמְפַרְנֵס וְעוֹנֶה וּמְרַחֵם |
| b'chöl ays tzöröh v'tzuköh, ayn lönu | בְּכָל עֵת צָרָה וְצוּקָה, אֵין לָנוּ |
| melech elö ötö, elohay hö-rishonim | מֶלֶךְ אֶלָּא אָתָּה, אֱלֹהֵי הָרִאשׁוֹנִים |
| v'hö-acharonim. Elo-ah köl b'ri-yos, | וְהָאַחֲרוֹנִים. אֱלוֹהַּ כָּל בְּרִיּוֹת, |

119

adon köl tolödos, ha-m'hulöl b'rov
ha-tishböchos, ha-m'nahayg olömo
b'chesed uv'ri-yosöv b'rachamim,
vadonöy hinay lo yönum v'lo yishön,
ha-m'orayr y'shaynim, v'ha-may-kitz
nirdömim, v'ha-maysi-ach il'mim,
v'hamatir asurim, v'ha-somaych
nof'lim, v'hazokayf k'fufim, l'chö
l'vad'chö anachnu modim. Ilu finu
mölay shiröh ka-yöm, ul'shonaynu
rinöh ka-hamon galöv, v'sif'sosaynu
shevach k'merchavay röki-ah,
v'aynaynu m'iros ka-shemesh
v'cha-yöray-ach, v'yödaynu f'rushos
k'nish'ray shömö-yim, v'raglaynu
kalos kö-a-yölos. Ayn önu maspikim
l'hodos l'chö adonöy elohaynu
vaylo-hay avosaynu, ul'vöraych es
sh'mechö al achas may-elef al'fay
alöfim, v'ribay r'vövos p'ömim,
ha-tovos nisim v'niflö-os she-ösisö
imönu v'im avosaynu mil'fönim:
Mimitzra-yim g'altönu, adonöy
elohaynu, mibays avödim p'disönu,
b'rö-öv zantönu, uv'sövö kilkaltönu,

אֲדוֹן כָּל תּוֹלָדוֹת, הַמְהֻלָּל בְּרֹב
הַתִּשְׁבָּחוֹת, הַמְנַהֵג עוֹלָמוֹ
בְּחֶסֶד וּבְרִיּוֹתָיו בְּרַחֲמִים,
וַיהֹוָה הִנֵּה לֹא יָנוּם וְלֹא יִישָׁן,
הַמְעוֹרֵר יְשֵׁנִים, וְהַמֵּקִיץ
נִרְדָּמִים, וְהַמֵּשִׂיחַ אִלְּמִים,
וְהַמַּתִּיר אֲסוּרִים, וְהַסּוֹמֵךְ
נוֹפְלִים, וְהַזּוֹקֵף כְּפוּפִים, לְךָ
לְבַדְּךָ אֲנַחְנוּ מוֹדִים. אִלּוּ פִינוּ
מָלֵא שִׁירָה כַיָּם, וּלְשׁוֹנֵנוּ
רִנָּה כַּהֲמוֹן גַּלָּיו, וְשִׂפְתוֹתֵינוּ
שֶׁבַח כְּמֶרְחֲבֵי רָקִיעַ,
וְעֵינֵינוּ מְאִירוֹת כַּשֶּׁמֶשׁ
וְכַיָּרֵחַ, וְיָדֵינוּ פְרוּשׂוֹת
כְּנִשְׁרֵי שָׁמָיִם, וְרַגְלֵינוּ
קַלּוֹת כָּאַיָּלוֹת. אֵין אָנוּ מַסְפִּיקִים
לְהוֹדוֹת לְךָ יְהֹוָה אֱלֹהֵינוּ
וֵאלֹהֵי אֲבוֹתֵינוּ, וּלְבָרֵךְ אֶת
שְׁמֶךָ עַל אַחַת מֵאֶלֶף אַלְפֵי
אֲלָפִים, וְרִבֵּי רְבָבוֹת פְּעָמִים,
הַטּוֹבוֹת נִסִּים וְנִפְלָאוֹת שֶׁעָשִׂיתָ
עִמָּנוּ וְעִם אֲבוֹתֵינוּ מִלְּפָנִים:
מִמִּצְרַיִם גְּאַלְתָּנוּ, יְהֹוָה
אֱלֹהֵינוּ, מִבֵּית עֲבָדִים פְּדִיתָנוּ,
בְּרָעָב זַנְתָּנוּ, וּבְשָׂבָע כִּלְכַּלְתָּנוּ,

**120**

may-cherev hitzaltönu, umidever
milat-tönu, umay-chölö-yim rö-im
v'ne-emönim dilisönu. Ad hay-nö
azörunu racha-mechö, v'lo azövunu
chasödechö, v'al tit'shaynu adonöy
elohaynu, löne-tzach. Al kayn,
ayvörim shepilagtö bönu, v'ru-ach
un'shömöh she-nöfachtö b'apaynu,
v'löshon asher samtö b'finu. Hayn
haym: Yodu vivö-r'chu vishab'chu
vifö-aru, viro-m'mu v'ya-ari-tzu,
v'yakdishu v'yamlichu es
shim'chö malkaynu. Ki chöl peh,
l'chö yo-deh. V'chöl löshon l'chö
si-shöva. V'chöl a-yin l'chö s'tza-peh.
V'chöl berech, l'chö sichra. V'chöl
komöh, l'fönechö sish-tachaveh.
V'chöl ha-l'vövos yirö-uchö.
V'chöl kerev uch'lö-yos y'zam'ru
lish'mechö, kadövör shekösuv,
köl atz'mosai tomarnöh: Adonöy,
mi chömochö, matzil öni maychözök
mimenu, v'öni v'ev-yon migoz'lo.
Mi yidmeh löch, umi yishveh löch,
umi ya-aröch löch, hö-ayl ha-gödol,

מֵחֶרֶב הִצַּלְתָּנוּ, וּמִדֶּבֶר
מִלַּטְתָּנוּ, וּמֵחֳלָיִם רָעִים
וְנֶאֱמָנִים דִּלִּיתָנוּ. עַד הֵנָּה
עֲזָרוּנוּ רַחֲמֶיךָ, וְלֹא עֲזָבוּנוּ
חֲסָדֶיךָ, וְאַל תִּטְּשֵׁנוּ יְהֹוָה
אֱלֹהֵינוּ, לָנֶצַח. עַל כֵּן,
אֵבָרִים שֶׁפִּלַּגְתָּ בָּנוּ, וְרוּחַ
וּנְשָׁמָה שֶׁנָּפַחְתָּ בְּאַפֵּינוּ,
וְלָשׁוֹן אֲשֶׁר שַׂמְתָּ בְּפִינוּ. הֵן
הֵם : יוֹדוּ וִיבָרְכוּ וִישַׁבְּחוּ
וִיפָאֲרוּ, וִירוֹמְמוּ וְיַעֲרִיצוּ,
וְיַקְדִּישׁוּ וְיַמְלִיכוּ אֶת
שִׁמְךָ מַלְכֵּנוּ. כִּי כָל פֶּה
לְךָ יוֹדֶה. וְכָל לָשׁוֹן לְךָ
תִשָּׁבַע. וְכָל עַיִן לְךָ תְצַפֶּה.
וְכָל בֶּרֶךְ, לְךָ תִכְרַע. וְכָל
קוֹמָה, לְפָנֶיךָ תִשְׁתַּחֲוֶה.
וְכָל הַלְּבָבוֹת יִירָאוּךָ.
וְכָל קֶרֶב וּכְלָיוֹת יְזַמְּרוּ
לִשְׁמֶךָ. כַּדָּבָר שֶׁכָּתוּב,
כָּל עַצְמוֹתַי תֹּאמַרְנָה : יְהֹוָה,
מִי כָמוֹךָ, מַצִּיל עָנִי מֵחָזָק
מִמֶּנּוּ, וְעָנִי וְאֶבְיוֹן מִגֹּזְלוֹ.
מִי יִדְמֶה לָּךְ, וּמִי יִשְׁוֶה לָּךְ,
וּמִי יַעֲרָךְ לָךְ, הָאֵל הַגָּדוֹל,

| | |
|---|---|
| ha-gibor v'ha-noröh, ayl el-yon konay | הַגִּבּוֹר וְהַנּוֹרָא, אֵל עֶלְיוֹן קֹנֵה |
| shöma-yim vö-öretz. N'halel'chö, | שָׁמַיִם וָאָרֶץ. נְהַלֶּלְךָ, |
| un'shabaychachö, un'fö-er'chö, | וּנְשַׁבֵּחֲךָ, וּנְפָאֶרְךָ, |
| un'völaych es shaym köd-shechö, | וּנְבָרֵךְ אֶת שֵׁם קָדְשֶׁךָ, |
| kö-ömur: L'dövid, bö-r'chi nafshi | כָּאָמוּר: לְדָוִד, בָּרְכִי נַפְשִׁי |
| es adonöy, v'chöl k'növai | אֶת יְהֹוָה, וְכָל קְרָבַי |
| es shaym köd-sho. | אֶת שֵׁם קָדְשׁוֹ: |

*The soul of every living being shall bless Your Name, Lord our God; and the spirit of all flesh shall continuously glorify and exalt Your remembrance, our King. From the highest world to the lowest, You are Almighty God; and aside from You we have no King, Redeemer and Savior Who delivers, rescues, sustains, answers, and is merciful in every time of distress and tribulation; we have no King other than You. [You are] the God of the first and of the last [generations], God of all created things, Master of all events, Who is extolled with manifold praises, Who directs His world with kindness and His creatures with compassion. Indeed, the Lord neither slumbers nor sleeps. It is He Who rouses those who sleep, Who awakens those who slumber, Who enables the mute to speak, Who releases the bound, Who supports those who fall, and Who makes erect those who are bowed. To You alone we offer thanks. Even if our mouth were filled with song as the sea [is filled with water], our tongue with melody as the roar of its waves, and our lips with praise as the breadth of the firmament; and our eyes were radiant like the sun and the moon, our hands spread out as the [wings of the] eagles of the sky, and our feet as swift as the deer – we would still be unable to thank You, Lord our God and God of our fathers, and bless Your Name for even one of the innumerable myriads of favors, miracles and wonders which You have performed for us and for our fathers before us. Lord our God, You have delivered us from Egypt, redeemed us from the house of bondage, sustained us in famine and nourished us in plenty,* rescued us from the sword and saved us from the plague, and kept us from severe and lasting maladies. Until now Your mercies have helped us, and Your kindnesses have not forsaken us; and You, Lord our God, will never abandon us. Therefore, the limbs which You have arranged within us, the spirit and soul which You have breathed into our nostrils, and the tongue which You have placed in our mouth – they all shall thank, bless, praise and glorify, exalt and adore, hallow and proclaim the sovereignty of Your Name, our King. For every mouth shall offer thanks to You, every tongue shall swear by Your Name, every eye shall look to You, every knee shall bend to You, all who stand erect shall prostrate themselves before You, all hearts shall fear You, and every innermost part shall sing to Your Name, as it is written: My entire being shall declare: Lord, who is like You; who saves the poor from one stronger than he, the poor and the destitute from one who would rob him! Who can be likened to You, who is equal to You, who can be compared to You, the great, mighty and awesome God, exalted God, Creator of heaven and earth! We will laud, extol and glorify You and bless Your holy Name, as it is said: [A Psalm] by David; bless the Lord, O my soul, and all my being – His holy Name.

| | |
|---|---|
| Hö-ayl b'sa-atzumos uzechö, ha-gödol | הָאֵל בְּתַעֲצֻמוֹת עֻזֶּךָ, הַגָּדוֹל |
| bich'vod sh'mecho, ha-gibor | בִּכְבוֹד שְׁמֶךָ, הַגִּבּוֹר |
| lö-ne-tzach, v'ha-norö b'nor'osechö. | לָנֶצַח, וְהַנּוֹרָא בְּנוֹרְאוֹתֶיךָ: |
| Ha-melech ha-yoshayv al kisay | הַמֶּלֶךְ הַיּוֹשֵׁב עַל כִּסֵּא |
| röm v'nisö. | רָם וְנִשָּׂא: |

*You are the Almighty by virtue of the strength of Your power; the Great by virtue of the glory of Your Name; the Powerful for eternity, and the Awesome by virtue of Your awe-inspiring deeds; O King Who sits upon a lofty and sublime throne.*

Shochayn ad, mörom v'ködosh
sh'mo, v'chösuv ran'nu tzadikim
badonöy, la-y'shörim növöh s'hilöh.
B'fi y'shörim tisro-möm, uv'sif'say
tzadikim tisböraych, uvil'shon
chasidim tiskadösh, uv'kerev
k'doshim tis-halöl.

שׁוֹכֵן עַד, מָרוֹם וְקָדוֹשׁ
שְׁמוֹ, וְכָתוּב רַנְּנוּ צַדִּיקִים
בַּיהוָה, לַיְשָׁרִים נָאוָה תְהִלָּה.
בְּפִי יְשָׁרִים תִּתְרוֹמָם, וּבְשִׂפְתֵי
צַדִּיקִים תִּתְבָּרֵךְ, וּבִלְשׁוֹן
חֲסִידִים תִּתְקַדָּשׁ, וּבְקֶרֶב
קְדוֹשִׁים תִּתְהַלָּל:

*He Who dwells for eternity, exalted and holy is His Name. And it is written: Sing joyously to the Lord, you righteous; it is fitting for the upright to offer praise. By the mouth of the upright You are exalted; by the lips of the righteous You are blessed; by the tongue of the pious You are hallowed; and in the innermost part of the holy ones You are praised.*

Uv'mak-haylos riv'vos am'chö bays
yisrö-ayl, b'rinöh yispö-ayr shim'chö
malkaynu b'chöl dor vödor. She-kayn
chovas köl ha-y'tzurim. L'fönechö
adonöy elohaynu vaylohay avosaynu:
L'hodos, l'halayl, l'shabay-ach,
l'fö-ayr, l'romaym, l'hadayr, l'vöraych,
l'alay ul'kalays, al köl div'ray
shiros v'sish-b'chos dövid ben
yishai av-d'chö, m'shi-chechö.

וּבְמַקְהֲלוֹת רִבְבוֹת עַמְּךָ בֵּית
יִשְׂרָאֵל, בְּרִנָּה יִתְפָּאֵר שִׁמְךָ
מַלְכֵּנוּ בְּכָל דּוֹר וָדוֹר, שֶׁכֵּן
חוֹבַת כָּל הַיְצוּרִים, לְפָנֶיךָ
יְהוָה אֱלֹהֵינוּ וֵאלֹהֵי אֲבוֹתֵינוּ:
לְהוֹדוֹת, לְהַלֵּל, לְשַׁבֵּחַ,
לְפָאֵר, לְרוֹמֵם, לְהַדֵּר, לְבָרֵךְ,
לְעַלֵּה וּלְקַלֵּס, עַל כָּל דִּבְרֵי
שִׁירוֹת וְתִשְׁבְּחוֹת דָּוִד בֶּן
יִשַׁי עַבְדְּךָ, מְשִׁיחֶךָ:

*In the assemblies of the myriads of Your people, the House of Israel, with song shall Your Name, our King, be glorified, in every generation. For that is the obligation of all created beings, Lord our God and God of our fathers, to offer thanks to You, to laud, to praise, to glorify, to exalt, to extol, to bless, to magnify and to acclaim You, even more than all the words of songs of praise and adorations of David, the son of Yishai, Your anointed servant.*

Uv'chayn yishtabach shim'chö lö-ad
malkaynu, hö-ayl, ha-melech
ha-gödol v'haködosh, ba-shöma-yim
uvö-öretz. Ki l'chö nö-eh adonöy
elohay-nu vay-lohay avosaynu l'olöm
vö-ed: Shir ush'vöchöh, ha-layl
v'zimröh, oz umemshölöh,
ne-tzach, g'dulöh ug'vuröh, t'hilöh
v'sif-eres, k'dushö umal'chus.
B'röchos v'hodö-os, l'shim'chö
ha-gödol v'ha-ködosh, umayolöm ad
olöm, atöh ayl. Böruch atöh adonöy,
ayl melech, gödol um'hulöl
batishböchos, ayl ha-hodö-os, adon
ha-niflö-os, boray köl ha-n'shömos,
ribon köl ha-ma-asim, ha-bochayr
b'shiray zimröh, melch yöchid
chay hö-olömim.

וּבְכֵן יִשְׁתַּבַּח שִׁמְךָ לָעַד
מַלְכֵּנוּ, הָאֵל הַמֶּלֶךְ
הַגָּדוֹל וְהַקָּדוֹשׁ, בַּשָּׁמַיִם
וּבָאָרֶץ. כִּי לְךָ נָאֶה יְהֹוָה
אֱלֹהֵינוּ וֵאלֹהֵי אֲבוֹתֵינוּ לְעוֹלָם
וָעֶד: שִׁיר וּשְׁבָחָה, הַלֵּל
וְזִמְרָה, עֹז וּמֶמְשָׁלָה,
נֶצַח, גְּדֻלָּה וּגְבוּרָה, תְּהִלָּה
וְתִפְאֶרֶת, קְדֻשָּׁה וּמַלְכוּת:
בְּרָכוֹת וְהוֹדָאוֹת, לְשִׁמְךָ
הַגָּדוֹל וְהַקָּדוֹשׁ, וּמֵעוֹלָם עַד
עוֹלָם, אַתָּה אֵל. בָּרוּךְ אַתָּה יְהֹוָה,
אֵל מֶלֶךְ, גָּדוֹל וּמְהֻלָּל
בַּתִּשְׁבָּחוֹת, אֵל הַהוֹדָאוֹת, אֲדוֹן
הַנִּפְלָאוֹת, בּוֹרֵא כָּל הַנְּשָׁמוֹת,
רִבּוֹן כָּל הַמַּעֲשִׂים, הַבּוֹחֵר
בְּשִׁירֵי זִמְרָה, מֶלֶךְ יָחִיד
חֵי הָעוֹלָמִים:

*And therefore may Your Name be praised forever, our King, the Almighty God, the great and holy King, in heaven and on earth. For to You, Lord our God and*

*God of our fathers, it is fitting forever to offer song and praise, adoration and melody, [to acclaim Your] might and dominion, victory, grandeur and power, glory, splendor, holiness and sovereignty; blessings and thanksgiving to Your great and holy Name; from the highest world to the lowest, You are God. Blessed are You Lord, Almighty God, great King, extolled with praises, God worthy of thanksgiving, Master of wonders, Creator of all souls, Ruler of all creatures, Who takes pleasure in songs of praise; You are the only King, the Life of [all] the worlds.*

Lift the cup with your right hand. Transfer it to the left hand. Lower it into the cupped palm of your right hand (if you write with your left hand, reverse). Lift the cup at least 3 inches above the table. Recite the blessing below.

Böruch atöh adonöy, elohaynu בָּרוּךְ אַתָּה יְיָ, אֱלֹהֵינוּ
melech hö-olöm, boray p'ri ha-göfen. מֶלֶךְ הָעוֹלָם, בּוֹרֵא פְּרִי הַגָּפֶן:

*Blessed are You, Lord our God, King of the universe, Who creates the fruit of the vine.*

Drink the fourth and last cup of wine (at least 3.5 ounces), while reclining to the left. After drinking the wine recite the following after-blessing.

Böruch atöh adonöy elohaynu בָּרוּךְ אַתָּה יְהֹוָה אֱלֹהֵינוּ
melech hö-olöm al hagefen v'al p'ri מֶלֶךְ הָעוֹלָם עַל הַגֶּפֶן וְעַל פְּרִי
hagefen v'al t'nuvas ha-sö-deh v'al הַגֶּפֶן וְעַל תְּנוּבַת הַשָּׂדֶה וְעַל
eretz chemdöh tovöh ur'chövöh אֶרֶץ חֶמְדָּה טוֹבָה וּרְחָבָה

| | |
|---|---|
| sherö-tzisö v'hin-chaltö la-avosaynu | שֶׁרָצִיתָ וְהִנְחַלְתָּ לַאֲבוֹתֵינוּ |
| le-echol mipir-yöh v'lisbo-a mituvö. | לֶאֱכוֹל מִפִּרְיָהּ וְלִשְׂבּוֹעַ מִטּוּבָהּ. |
| Rachem nö adonöy elohaynu al | רַחֶם נָא יְהֹוָה אֱלֹהֵינוּ עַל |
| yisrö-ayl amechö v'al y'rushöla-yim | יִשְׂרָאֵל עַמֶּךָ וְעַל יְרוּשָׁלַיִם |
| irechö v'al tziyon mishkan k'vodechö | עִירֶךָ וְעַל צִיּוֹן מִשְׁכַּן כְּבוֹדֶךָ |
| v'al miz-b'chechö v'al hay-chölechö | וְעַל מִזְבְּחֶךָ וְעַל הֵיכָלֶךָ |
| uv'nay y'rushöla-yim ir ha-kodesh | וּבְנֵה יְרוּשָׁלַיִם עִיר הַקֹּדֶשׁ |
| bim'hayröh v'yömaynu v'ha-alaynu | בִּמְהֵרָה בְיָמֵינוּ וְהַעֲלֵנוּ |
| l'sochöh, v'sam'chaynu vöh | לְתוֹכָהּ, וְשַׂמְּחֵנוּ בָהּ |
| un'vörech'chö bik'dushö uv'töhöröh, | וּנְבָרֶכְךָ בִּקְדֻשָׁה וּבְטָהֳרָה, |
| (On Shabbat add: | בשבת: |
| ur'tzay v'hachali-tzaynu b'yom | וּרְצֵה וְהַחֲלִיצֵנוּ בְּיוֹם |
| b'yom has-habös ha-zeh.) | הַשַּׁבָּת הַזֶּה. |
| v'zöch'raynu l'tovöh b'yom chag | וְזָכְרֵנוּ לְטוֹבָה בְּיוֹם חַג |
| ha-matzos ha-zeh. Ki atöh adonöy tov | הַמַּצּוֹת הַזֶּה. כִּי אַתָּה יְהֹוָה טוֹב |
| umaytiv lakol v'no-deh l'chö al | וּמֵטִיב לַכֹּל וְנוֹדֶה לְךָ עַל |
| hö-öretz v'al p'ri ha-göfen. | הָאָרֶץ וְעַל פְּרִי הַגָּפֶן. |
| Böruch atöh adonöy, | בָּרוּךְ אַתָּה יְהֹוָה, |
| al hö-öretz v'al p'ri ha-göfen. | עַל הָאָרֶץ וְעַל פְּרִי הַגָּפֶן: |

*Blessed are You, Lord our God, King of the universe, for the vine and the fruit of the vine, for the produce of the field, and for the precious, good and spacious land which You have graciously given as a heritage to our ancestors, to eat of its fruit and be satiated with its goodness. Have mercy, Lord our God, on Israel Your people, on Jerusalem Your city, on Zion the abode of Your glory, on Your altar and on Your Temple. Rebuild Jerusalem, the holy city, speedily in our days, and* bring us up to it and make us rejoice in it, and we will bless You in holiness and purity. (On Shabbat: May it please You to strengthen us on this Shabbat day.) Remember us for good on this day of the Festival of Matzot. For You, Lord, are good and do good to all, and we offer thanks to You for the land and for the fruit of the vine. Blessed are You Lord, for the land and for the fruit of the vine.

Having carried out the seder service properly, we are sure that it has been well received by the Almighty. We conclude the seder with the following prayer and proclamation:

L'shönö ha-bö-öh biru-shölö-yim.　לְשָׁנָה הַבָּאָה בִּירוּשָׁלָיִם:

*Next Year in Jerusalem!*

# Kiddush for Passover Day

On the first and last two days of Passover we recite the following *Kiddush* for the afternoon meal.

| | |
|---|---|
| Askinu s'udöso d'malkö | אַתְקִינוּ סְעוּדָתָא דְמַלְכָּא |
| sh'laymöso chedvöso d'malkö | שְׁלֵימָתָא חֶדְוָתָא דְמַלְכָּא |
| ka-dishö dö hi s'udöso d'kud'shö | קַדִּישָׁא דָא הִיא סְעוּדָתָא דְּקוּדְשָׁא |
| b'rich hu ush'chintay. | בְּרִיךְ הוּא וּשְׁכִינְתֵּיהּ׃ |

*Prepare the meal of the King, the complete delight of the Holy King. This is the meal of the Holy One, blessed be He, and His Shechinah. (Ed.: Kabbalistic term for a manifestation of God's presence).*

## Directions for the Kiddush

The Kiddush is recited standing, with a cup of wine or grape juice containing at least 3.5 fluid ounces. Lift the cup with your right hand. Transfer it to the left hand. Lower it into the cupped palm of your right hand (if you write with your left hand, reverse). Lift the cup at least 3 inches above the table. Recite the blessings below.

| | |
|---|---|
| Ay-leh mo-aday adonöy mikrö-ay | אֵלֶּה מוֹעֲדֵי יְיָ מִקְרָאֵי |
| kodesh asher tik-r'u osöm | קֹדֶשׁ אֲשֶׁר תִּקְרְאוּ אֹתָם |
| b'mo-adöm. **Continue below.** | בְּמוֹעֲדָם׃ |

*These are the Festivals of the Lord, holy assemblies, which you shall proclaim at their appointed times.*

Savri mörönön: Böruch atöh adonöy, סַבְרִי מָרָנָן: בָּרוּךְ אַתָּה יְיָ,
elohaynu melech hö-olöm, אֱלֹהֵינוּ מֶלֶךְ הָעוֹלָם,
boray p'ri ha-göfen. בּוֹרֵא פְּרִי הַגָּפֶן:

*Attention, gentlemen! Blessed are You, Lord our God, King of the universe, Who creates the fruit of the vine.*

Sit and drink at least 2 ounces from the cup. Distibute some wine to everyone present. Proceed with the washing of the hands for matzah (below).

# Procedure for
# Washing the Hands for Matzah

Remove any rings. Fill a large cup with at least 3.5 ounces of cold water, while holding it in your right hand. Transfer the cup to your left hand and pour three times over your whole right hand. Transfer it to your right hand and pour three times over your whole left hand. Rub your hands together and recite the blessing below. Then dry your hands.

Böruch atöh adonöy elohaynu בָּרוּךְ אַתָּה יְיָ אֱלֹהֵינוּ
melech hö-olöm, asher kid'shönu מֶלֶךְ הָעוֹלָם, אֲשֶׁר קִדְּשָׁנוּ
b'mitzvosöv, v'tzivönu בְּמִצְוֹתָיו, וְצִוָּנוּ
al n'tilas yödö-yim. עַל נְטִילַת יָדָיִם:

*Blessed are You, Lord our God, King of the universe, Who has sanctified us with His commandments, and commanded us concerning the washing of the hands.*

Do not talk until you have made the blessing and have eaten a piece of matzah. Uncover the two matzot. Hold both matzot in your hand. Recite the following blessing:

בָּרוּךְ אַתָּה יְיָ אֱלֹהֵינוּ
מֶלֶךְ הָעוֹלָם,
הַמּוֹצִיא לֶחֶם מִן הָאָרֶץ:

Böruch atöh adonöy
elohaynu melech hö-olöm,
hamotzi lechem min hö-öretz.

*Blessed are You, Lord our God, King of the universe, Who brings forth bread from the earth.*

Break off a piece and eat. Pass additional pieces around to the assembled family and guests.

# Popular Passover Songs

The festive holiday table experience is a very special one as we all radiate the special warmth of the day. To prime and amplify this joy we have included many popular songs below. Sing to your hearts' content!

**1.** Avödim hö-yinu l'far-oh
b'mitzrö-yim va-yo-tzi-aynu hashem
elokaynu mishöm b'yöd chazököh
uviz'ro-ah n'tu-yöh.

עֲבָדִים הָיִינוּ לְפַרְעֹה
בְּמִצְרָיִם וַיּוֹצִיאֵנוּ ה'
אֱלֹקֵינוּ מִשָּׁם בְּיָד חֲזָקָה
וּבִזְרוֹעַ נְטוּיָה.

*We were slaves to Pharaoh in Egypt, and the Lord our God took us out from there with a strong hand and an outstretched arm.*

**2.** V'hi she-ö-m'döh la-avosaynu
v'lönu shelo echöd bil'vöd
ömad ölaynu l'chalo-saynu elö
sheb'chöl dor vödor om'dim
ölaynu l'chalo-saynu. V'haködosh
böruch hu matzilaynu mi-yödöm.

וְהִיא שֶׁעָמְדָה לַאֲבוֹתֵינוּ
וְלָנוּ. שֶׁלֹּא אֶחָד בִּלְבָד
עָמַד עָלֵינוּ לְכַלּוֹתֵנוּ אֶלָּא
שֶׁבְּכָל דּוֹר וָדוֹר עוֹמְדִים
עָלֵינוּ לְכַלּוֹתֵנוּ. וְהַקָּדוֹשׁ
בָּרוּךְ הוּא מַצִּילֵנוּ מִיָּדָם.

*It is this that has stood by our fathers and us. For not only one has risen against us to annihilate us, but in every generation they rise against us to annihilate us. But the Holy One, Blessed be He, rescues us from their hand.*

**132**

**3.** Ilu hotzi-önu אִלּוּ הוֹצִיאָנוּ
mimitzra-yim da-yaynu. מִמִּצְרַיִם דַּיֵּנוּ.

*Had He [only] brought us out of Egypt, it would have sufficed us.*

**4.** Al achas kamöh עַל אַחַת כַּמָּה
v'chamöh tovöh ch'fulöh וְכַמָּה טוֹבָה כְפוּלָה
um'chupeles la-mökom ölaynu. וּמְכֻפֶּלֶת לַמָּקוֹם עָלֵינוּ.
She-ho-tzi-önu mimitzrö-yim. שֶׁהוֹצִיאָנוּ מִמִּצְרָיִם.

*Thus, how much more so [do we owe thanks] to the Omnipresent for the repeated and manifold favors He bestowed upon us: He brought us out of Egypt.*

**5.** Kayli atöh v'odekö קֵלִי אַתָּה וְאוֹדֶךָּ
elokai aro-m'mekö. אֱלֹקַי אֲרוֹמְמֶךָּ.

*You are my God and I will praise you, my God and I will exalt You.*

**6.** Ayli-yöhu ha-növi, ayli-yöhu אֵלִיָּהוּ הַנָּבִיא, אֵלִיָּהוּ
ha-tishbi, ayli-yöhu ha-gil-ödi, הַתִּשְׁבִּי, אֵלִיָּהוּ הַגִּלְעָדִי,
bim'hayröh yövo aylaynu im בִּמְהֵרָה יָבֹא אֵלֵינוּ עִם
möshi-ach ben dövid. מָשִׁיחַ בֶּן דָּוִד.

*Elijah the prophet, Elijah the Tishbi, Elijah the Gilodi, will swiftly come to us with Moshiach the son of David.*

**7.** Chasal siddur pesach k'hil'chöso. חֲסַל סִדּוּר פֶּסַח כְּהִלְכָתוֹ.
K'chöl mishpöto v'chuköso. Ka-asher כְּכָל מִשְׁפָּטוֹ וְחֻקָּתוֹ. כַּאֲשֶׁר

zöchinu l'sadayr oso. Kayn nizkeh    זָכִינוּ לְסַדֵּר אוֹתוֹ. כֵּן נִזְכֶּה

la-asoso. Zöch sho-chayn m'onöh.    לַעֲשׂוֹתוֹ. זָךְ שׁוֹכֵן מְעוֹנָה.

Komaym k'hal adas mi mönöh.    קוֹמֵם קְהַל עֲדַת מִי מָנָה.

B'körov na-hayl nit'ay chanöh.    בְּקָרוֹב נַהֵל נִטְעֵי כַנָּה.

P'du-yim l'tzi-yon b'rinöh.    פְּדוּיִם לְצִיּוֹן בְּרִנָּה׃

*The Pesach seder has been completed in accordance with its law, with all its rules and statutes; just as we merited to observe it, so may we merit to perform it again. Pure One, Who dwells on high, raise up the congregation that is without number! Soon may You lead the stock You have planted, redeemed to Zion in joyous song.*

8. L'shönö ha-bö-öh    לְשָׁנָה הַבָּאָה

     birushölö-yim.    בִּירוּשָׁלָיִם׃

*Next Year in Jerusalem!*

9. Ki lo nö-eh. Ki lo yö-eh.    כִּי לוֹ נָאֶה. כִּי לוֹ יָאֶה.

     Adir bim'luchöh. Böchur    אַדִּיר בִּמְלוּכָה. בָּחוּר

ka-ha-lö-chöh. G'dudöv yom'ru lo.    כַּהֲלָכָה. גְּדוּדָיו יֹאמְרוּ לוֹ.

L'chö ul'chö. L'chö ki l'chö. L'chö af    לְךָ וּלְךָ. לְךָ כִּי לְךָ. לְךָ אַף

l'chö. L'chö hashem ha-mam-löchöh.    לְךָ. לְךָ ה׳ הַמַּמְלָכָה.

Ki lo nö-eh. Ki lo yö-eh.    כִּי לוֹ נָאֶה. כִּי לוֹ יָאֶה.

Dögul bim'luchöh. Hö-dur    דָּגוּל בִּמְלוּכָה. הָדוּר

ka-ha-löchöh. Vö-siköv yom'ru lo. לְךָ    כַּהֲלָכָה. וָתִיקָיו יֹאמְרוּ לוֹ.

Zakai bim'luchöh. Chösin | זַכַּאי בִּמְלוּכָה. חָסִין
ka-ha-löchöh. Tafs'röv yom'ru lo. | כַּהֲלָכָה. טַפְסְרָיו יֹאמְרוּ לוֹ. לְךָ

Yöchid bim'luchöh. Kabir | יָחִיד בִּמְלוּכָה. כַּבִּיר
ka-ha-löchöh. Limudöv yom'ru lo. | כַּהֲלָכָה. לִמּוּדָיו יֹאמְרוּ לוֹ. לְךָ

Mo-shayl bim'luchöh. Noröh | מוֹשֵׁל בִּמְלוּכָה. נוֹרָא
ka-ha-löchöh. S'vivöv yom'ru lo. | כַּהֲלָכָה. סְבִיבָיו יֹאמְרוּ לוֹ. לְךָ

Önöv bim'luchöh. Podeh | עָנָו בִּמְלוּכָה. פּוֹדֶה
ka-ha-löchöh. Tzadiköv yom'ru lo. | כַּהֲלָכָה. צַדִּיקָיו יֹאמְרוּ לוֹ. לְךָ

Ködosh bim'luchöh. Rachum | קָדוֹשׁ בִּמְלוּכָה. רַחוּם
ka-ha-löchöh. Shin-anöv yom'ru lo. | כַּהֲלָכָה. שִׁנְאַנָּיו יֹאמְרוּ לוֹ. לְךָ

Takif bim'luchöh. Tomaych | תַּקִּיף בִּמְלוּכָה. תּוֹמֵךְ
ka-ha-löchöh. T'mimöv yom'ru lo. | כַּהֲלָכָה. תְּמִימָיו יֹאמְרוּ לוֹ. לְךָ

*To Him, praise is pleasant; to Him, praise is due! Mighty in Kingship, truly distinguished, His legions say to Him: To You and only You, to You and just for You, to You, yes, only You, to You, God, Kingship is due, to Him, praise is pleasant; to Him, praise is due.*

**10.** Adir hu. Yivneh vayso b'körov. | אַדִּיר הוּא. יִבְנֶה בֵיתוֹ בְּקָרוֹב.
Bim'hayröh bim'hayröh b'yömaynu | בִּמְהֵרָה בִּמְהֵרָה בְּיָמֵינוּ
b'körov. Kayl b'nay. Kayl b'nay. | בְּקָרוֹב. קֵל בְּנֵה. קֵל בְּנֵה.
B'nay vays'chö b'korov. | בְּנֵה בֵיתְךָ בְּקָרוֹב:

Böchur hu. Gödol hu. Dögul hu. | בָּחוּר הוּא. גָּדוֹל הוּא. דָּגוּל הוּא.

| | |
|---|---|
| Yivneh vayso b'körov. Bim'hayröh | יִבְנֶה בֵיתוֹ בְּקָרוֹב. בִּמְהֵרָה |
| bim'hayröh b'yömaynu b'körov. | בִּמְהֵרָה בְּיָמֵינוּ בְּקָרוֹב. |
| Kayl b'nay. Kayl b'nay. B'nay | קֵל בְּנֵה. קֵל בְּנֵה. בְּנֵה |
| vays'chö b'korov. | בֵיתְךָ בְּקָרוֹב : |

| | |
|---|---|
| Hödur hu. Vösik hu. Zakai hu. | הָדוּר הוּא. וָתִיק הוּא. זַכַּאי הוּא. |
| Chösid hu. Yivneh vayso b'körov. | חָסִיד הוּא. יִבְנֶה בֵיתוֹ בְּקָרוֹב. |
| Bim'hayröh bim'hayröh b'yömaynu | בִּמְהֵרָה בִּמְהֵרָה בְּיָמֵינוּ |
| b'körov. Kayl b'nay. Kayl b'nay. | בְּקָרוֹב. קֵל בְּנֵה. קֵל בְּנֵה. |
| B'nay vays'chö b'korov. | בְּנֵה בֵיתְךָ בְּקָרוֹב : |

| | |
|---|---|
| Töhor hu. Yöchid hu. Kabir hu. | טָהוֹר הוּא. יָחִיד הוּא. כַּבִּיר הוּא. |
| Lömud hu. Melech hu. Noröh hu. | לָמוּד הוּא. מֶלֶךְ הוּא. נוֹרָא הוּא. |
| Sagiv hu. Izuz hu. Po-deh hu. | סַגִּיב הוּא. עִזּוּז הוּא. פּוֹדֶה הוּא. |
| Tzadik hu. Yivneh vayso b'körov. | צַדִּיק הוּא. יִבְנֶה בֵיתוֹ בְּקָרוֹב. |
| Bim'hayröh bim'hayröh b'yömaynu | בִּמְהֵרָה בִּמְהֵרָה בְּיָמֵינוּ |
| b'körov. Kayl b'nay. Kayl b'nay. | בְּקָרוֹב. קֵל בְּנֵה. קֵל בְּנֵה. |
| B'nay vays'chö b'korov. | בְּנֵה בֵיתְךָ בְּקָרוֹב : |

| | |
|---|---|
| Ködosh hu. Rachum hu. Sha-kai hu | קָדוֹשׁ הוּא. רַחוּם הוּא. שַׁקַּי הוּא. |
| Takif hu. Yivneh vayso b'körov. | תַּקִּיף הוּא. יִבְנֶה בֵיתוֹ בְּקָרוֹב. |
| Bim'hayröh bim'hayröh b'yömaynu | בִּמְהֵרָה בִּמְהֵרָה בְּיָמֵינוּ |
| b'körov. Kayl b'nay. Kayl b'nay. | בְּקָרוֹב. קֵל בְּנֵה. קֵל בְּנֵה. |
| B'nay vays'chö b'korov. | בְּנֵה בֵיתְךָ בְּקָרוֹב : |

*He is Mighty. May He build His House soon. Quickly, quickly, soon in our days.*

**11.** Echöd mi yoday-a. Echöd ani yoday-a. Echöd elokaynu she-bashöma-yim uvö-öretz.

אֶחָד מִי יוֹדֵעַ. אֶחָד אֲנִי יוֹדֵעַ. אֶחָד אֱלֹקֵינוּ שֶׁבַּשָּׁמַיִם וּבָאָרֶץ :

Sh'na-yim mi yo-day-a. Sh'na-yim ani yoday-a. Sh'nay luchos ha-b'ris. Echöd elokaynu she-bashöma-yim uvö-öretz.

שְׁנַיִם מִי יוֹדֵעַ. שְׁנַיִם אֲנִי יוֹדֵעַ. שְׁנֵי לֻחוֹת הַבְּרִית. אֶחָד אֱלֹקֵינוּ שֶׁבַּשָּׁמַיִם וּבָאָרֶץ :

Sh'loshöh mi yoday-a. Sh'loshöh ani yoday-a. Sh'loshöh övos. Sh'nay luchos ha-b'ris. Echöd elokaynu she-bashöma-yim uvö-öretz.

שְׁלֹשָׁה מִי יוֹדֵעַ. שְׁלֹשָׁה אֲנִי יוֹדֵעַ. שְׁלֹשָׁה אָבוֹת. שְׁנֵי לֻחוֹת הַבְּרִית. אֶחָד אֱלֹקֵינוּ שֶׁבַּשָּׁמַיִם וּבָאָרֶץ :

Arba mi yoday-a. Arba ani yoday-a. Arba imö-hos. Sh'loshöh övos. Sh'nay luchos ha-b'ris. Echöd elokaynu she-bashöma-yim uvö-öretz.

אַרְבַּע מִי יוֹדֵעַ. אַרְבַּע אֲנִי יוֹדֵעַ. אַרְבַּע אִמָּהוֹת. שְׁלֹשָׁה אָבוֹת. שְׁנֵי לֻחוֹת הַבְּרִית. אֶחָד אֱלֹקֵינוּ שֶׁבַּשָּׁמַיִם וּבָאָרֶץ :

Chamishöh mi yiday-a. Chmishöh ani yoday-a. Chamishöh chum'shay soröh. Arba imö-hos. Sh'loshöh övos. Sh'nay luchos ha-b'ris. Echöd elokaynu she-bashöma-yim uvö-öretz.

חֲמִשָּׁה מִי יוֹדֵעַ. חֲמִשָּׁה אֲנִי יוֹדֵעַ. חֲמִשָּׁה חֻמְשֵׁי תוֹרָה. אַרְבַּע אִמָּהוֹת. שְׁלֹשָׁה אָבוֹת. שְׁנֵי לֻחוֹת הַבְּרִית. אֶחָד אֱלֹקֵינוּ שֶׁבַּשָּׁמַיִם וּבָאָרֶץ :

Shishöh mi yiday-a. Shishöh ani yoday-a. Shishöh sid'ray mishnöh. Chamishöh chum'shay

שִׁשָּׁה מִי יוֹדֵעַ. שִׁשָּׁה אֲנִי יוֹדֵעַ. שִׁשָּׁה סִדְרֵי מִשְׁנָה. חֲמִשָּׁה חֻמְשֵׁי

**137**

| | |
|---|---|
| soröh. Arba imö-hos. Sh'loshöh övos. Sh'nay luchos ha-b'ris. Echöd elokaynu she-bashöma-yim uvö-öretz. | שְׁלֹשָׁה אִמָּהוֹת. אַרְבַּע תּוֹרָה. אֶחָד הַבְּרִית. לֻחוֹת שְׁנֵי אָבוֹת. אֶלֹקֵינוּ שֶׁבַּשָּׁמַיִם וּבָאָרֶץ : |
| Shiv-öh mi yoday-a. Shiv-öh ani yoday-a. Shiv-öh y'may sha-batöh. Shishöh sid'ray mishnöh. Chamishöh chum'shay soröh. Arba imö-hos. Sh'loshöh övos. Sh'nay luchos ha-b'ris. Echöd elokaynu she-bashöma-yim uvö-öretz. | אֲנִי שִׁבְעָה יוֹדֵעַ. מִי שִׁבְעָה שַׁבַּתָּא. יְמֵי שִׁבְעָה יוֹדֵעַ. חֲמִשָּׁה מִשְׁנָה. סִדְרֵי שִׁשָּׁה אַרְבַּע אִמָּהוֹת. תּוֹרָה. חֻמְשֵׁי לֻחוֹת שְׁנֵי אָבוֹת. שְׁלֹשָׁה אֱלֹקֵינוּ אֶחָד הַבְּרִית. שֶׁבַּשָּׁמַיִם וּבָאָרֶץ : |
| Sh'monöh mi yoday-a. Sh'monöh ani yoday-a. Sh'monöh y'may milöh. Shiv-öh y'may sha-batöh. Shishöh sid'ray mishnöh. Chamishöh chum'shay soröh. Arba imö-hos. Sh'loshöh övos. Sh'nay luchos ha-b'ris. Echöd elokaynu she-bashöma-yim uvö-öretz. | אֲנִי שְׁמוֹנָה יוֹדֵעַ. מִי שְׁמוֹנָה מִילָה. יְמֵי שְׁמוֹנָה יוֹדֵעַ. שִׁשָּׁה שַׁבַּתָּא. יְמֵי שִׁבְעָה חֲמִשָּׁה מִשְׁנָה. סִדְרֵי אִמָּהוֹת. אַרְבַּע תּוֹרָה. חֻמְשֵׁי לֻחוֹת שְׁנֵי אָבוֹת. שְׁלֹשָׁה אֱלֹקֵינוּ אֶחָד הַבְּרִית. שֶׁבַּשָּׁמַיִם וּבָאָרֶץ : |
| Tish-öh mi yoday-a. Tish-öh ani yoday-a. Tish-öh yar'chay laydöh. Sh'monöh y'may milöh. Shiv-öh y'may sha-batöh. Shishöh sid'ray mishnöh. Chamishöh chum'shay | אֲנִי תִּשְׁעָה יוֹדֵעַ. מִי תִּשְׁעָה לֵידָה. יַרְחֵי תִּשְׁעָה יוֹדֵעַ. שִׁבְעָה מִילָה. יְמֵי שְׁמוֹנָה סִדְרֵי שִׁשָּׁה שַׁבַּתָּא. יְמֵי חֲמִשָּׁה חֲמִשָּׁה מִשְׁנָה. |

soröh. Arba imö-hos. Sh'loshöh övos. Sh'nay luchos ha-bris. Echöd elokaynu she-bashöma-yim uvö-öretz.

תּוֹרָה. אַרְבַּע אִמָּהוֹת. שְׁלֹשָׁה אָבוֹת. שְׁנֵי לֻחוֹת הַבְּרִית. אֶחָד אֱלֹקֵינוּ שֶׁבַּשָּׁמַיִם וּבָאָרֶץ :

Asöröh mi yoday a. Asöröh ani yoday-a. Asöröh dib'ra-yö. Tish-öh yar'chay laydöh. Sh'monöh y'may milöh. Shiv-öh y'may sha-batöh. Shishöh sid'ray mishnöh. Chamishöh chum'shay soröh. Arba imö-hos. Sh'loshöh övos. Sh'nay luchos ha-b'ris. Echöd elokaynu she-bashöma-yim uvö-öretz.

עֲשָׂרָה מִי יוֹדֵעַ. עֲשָׂרָה אֲנִי יוֹדֵעַ. עֲשָׂרָה דִּבְּרַיָּא. תִּשְׁעָה יַרְחֵי לֵידָה. שְׁמוֹנָה יְמֵי מִילָה. שִׁבְעָה יְמֵי שַׁבַּתָּא. שִׁשָּׁה סִדְרֵי מִשְׁנָה. חֲמִשָּׁה חֻמְשֵׁי תוֹרָה. אַרְבַּע אִמָּהוֹת. שְׁלֹשָׁה אָבוֹת. שְׁנֵי לֻחוֹת הַבְּרִית. אֶחָד אֱלֹקֵינוּ שֶׁבַּשָּׁמַיִם וּבָאָרֶץ :

Achad ösör mi yoday-a. Achad ösör ani yoday-a. Achad ösör koch'va-yö. Asöröh dib'ra-yö. Tish-öh yar'chay laydöh. Sh'monöh y'may milöh. Shiv-öh y'may sha-batöh. Shishöh sid'ray mishnöh.Chamishöh chum'shay soröh. Arba imö-hos. Sh'loshöh övos. Sh'nay luchos ha-b'ris. Echöd elokaynu she-bashöma-yim uvö-öretz.

אַחַד עָשָׂר מִי יוֹדֵעַ. אַחַד עָשָׂר אֲנִי יוֹדֵעַ. אַחַד עָשָׂר כּוֹכְבַיָּא. עֲשָׂרָה דִּבְּרַיָּא. תִּשְׁעָה יַרְחֵי לֵידָה. שְׁמוֹנָה יְמֵי מִילָה. שִׁבְעָה יְמֵי שַׁבַּתָּא. שִׁשָּׁה סִדְרֵי מִשְׁנָה. חֲמִשָּׁה חֻמְשֵׁי תוֹרָה. אַרְבַּע אִמָּהוֹת. שְׁלֹשָׁה אָבוֹת. שְׁנֵי לֻחוֹת הַבְּרִית. אֶחָד אֱלֹקֵינוּ שֶׁבַּשָּׁמַיִם וּבָאָרֶץ :

Sh'naym ösör mi yoday-a. Sh'naym ösör ani yoday-a. Sh'naym ösör shiv'ta-yö. Achad ösör koch'va-yö.Asöröh dibra-yö. Tish-öh yar'chay laydöh. Sh'monöh y'may milöh. Shiv-öh y'may sha-batöh. Shishöh sid'ray mishnöh.Chamishöh chum'shay soröh. Arba imö-hos. Sh'loshöh övos. Sh'nay luchos ha-b'ris. Echöd elokaynu she-bashöma-yim uvö-öretz.

שְׁנֵים עָשָׂר מִי יוֹדֵעַ. שְׁנֵים עָשָׂר אֲנִי יוֹדֵעַ. שְׁנֵים עָשָׂר שִׁבְטַיָּא. אַחַד עָשָׂר כּוֹכְבַיָּא. עֲשָׂרָה דִבְּרַיָּא. תִּשְׁעָה יַרְחֵי לֵידָה. שְׁמוֹנָה יְמֵי מִילָה. שִׁבְעָה יְמֵי שַׁבַּתָּא. שִׁשָּׁה סִדְרֵי מִשְׁנָה. חֲמִשָּׁה חֻמְשֵׁי תוֹרָה. אַרְבַּע אִמָּהוֹת. שְׁלֹשָׁה אָבוֹת. שְׁנֵי לֻחוֹת הַבְּרִית. אֶחָד אֱלֹקֵינוּ שֶׁבַּשָּׁמַיִם וּבָאָרֶץ :

Sh'loshöh ösör mi yoday-a. Sh'loshöh ösör ani yoday-a. Sh'loshöh ösör mida-yö. Sh'naym ösör shiv'ta-yö. Achad ösör koch'va-yö. Asöröh dib'ra-yö. Tish-öh yar'chay laydöh. Sh'monöh y'may milöh. Shiv-öh y'may sha-batöh. Shishöh sid'ray mishnöh. Chamishöh chum'shay soröh. Arba imö-hos. Shloshöh övos. Sh'nay luchos ha-b'ris. Echöd elokaynu she-bashöma-yim uvö-öretz.

שְׁלֹשָׁה עָשָׂר מִי יוֹדֵעַ. שְׁלֹשָׁה עָשָׂר אֲנִי יוֹדֵעַ. שְׁלֹשָׁה עָשָׂר מִדַּיָּא. שְׁנֵים עָשָׂר שִׁבְטַיָּא. אַחַד עָשָׂר כּוֹכְבַיָּא. עֲשָׂרָה דִבְּרַיָּא. תִּשְׁעָה יַרְחֵי לֵידָה. שְׁמוֹנָה יְמֵי מִילָה. שִׁבְעָה יְמֵי שַׁבַּתָּא. שִׁשָּׁה סִדְרֵי מִשְׁנָה. חֲמִשָּׁה חֻמְשֵׁי תוֹרָה. אַרְבַּע אִמָּהוֹת. שְׁלֹשָׁה אָבוֹת. שְׁנֵי לֻחוֹת הַבְּרִית. אֶחָד אֱלֹקֵינוּ שֶׁבַּשָּׁמַיִם וּבָאָרֶץ :

*Who knows one? I know one. One is our God in the heavens and on the earth.*
*Who knows two? I know two. Two are the Tablets of the Covenant (the Ten*

Commandments)... Who knows three? I know three. Three are the Patriarchs... Who knows four? I know four. Four are the Matriarchs... Who knows five? I know five. Five are the books of the Torah... Who knows six? I know six. Six are the orders of the Mishnah... Who knows seven? I know seven. Seven are the days of the week... Who knows eight? I know eight. Eight are the days of circumcision... Who knows nine? I know nine. Nine are the months of pregnancy... Who knows ten? I know ten. Ten are the Ten Commandments... Who knows eleven? I know eleven. Eleven are the stars [in Yoseph's dream]... Who knows twelve? I know twelve. Twelve are the tribes [of Israel]... Who knows thirteen? I know thirteen. Thirteen are God's attributes [of mercy].

12. Chad gad-yö. Chad gad-yö.    חַד גַּדְיָא. חַד גַּדְיָא.
     D'zabin aböh bis'ray zuzay.    דְּזַבִּין אַבָּא בִּתְרֵי זוּזֵי.
     Chad gad-yö. Chad gad-yö.    חַד גַּדְיָא. חַד גַּדְיָא :

     V'ösö shunrö v'och'löh l'gad-yö.    וְאָתָא שׁוּנְרָא וְאָכְלָה לְגַדְיָא.
     D'zabin aböh bis'ray zuzay.    דְּזַבִּין אַבָּא בִּתְרֵי זוּזֵי.
     Chad gad-yö. Chad gad-yö.    חַד גַּדְיָא. חַד גַּדְיָא :

     V'ösö chalbö v'nöshach    וְאָתָא כַלְבָּא וְנָשַׁךְ
     l'shunrö. D'öch'löh l'gad-yö.    לְשׁוּנְרָא. דְּאָכְלָה לְגַדְיָא.
     D'zabin aböh bis'ray zuzay.    דְּזַבִּין אַבָּא בִּתְרֵי זוּזֵי.
     Chad gad-yö. Chad gad-yö.    חַד גַּדְיָא. חַד גַּדְיָא :

     V'ösö chutrö v'hiköh l'chalbö.    וְאָתָא חוּטְרָא וְהִכָּה לְכַלְבָּא.
     D'nöshach l'shunrö. D'öch'löh    דְּנָשַׁךְ לְשׁוּנְרָא. דְּאָכְלָה

l'gad-yö. D'zabin aböh bis'ray zuzay.  לְגַדְיָא. דְּזַבִּין אַבָּא בִּתְרֵי זוּזֵי.
Chad gad-yö. Chad gad-yö.  חַד גַּדְיָא. חַד גַּדְיָא :

V'ösö nurö v'söraf l'chutröh.  וְאָתָא נוּרָא וְשָׂרַף לְחוּטְרָא.
D'hiköh l'chalbö. D'nöshach  דְּהִכָּה לְכַלְבָּא. דְּנָשַׁךְ
l'shunrö. D'öch'löh l'gad-yö.  לְשׁוּנְרָא. דְּאָכְלָה לְגַדְיָא.
D'zabin aböh bis'ray zuzay.  דְּזַבִּין אַבָּא בִּתְרֵי זוּזֵי.
Chad gad-yö. Chad gad-yö.  חַד גַּדְיָא. חַד גַּדְיָא :

V'ösö ma-yöh v'chövö l'nuröh.  וְאָתָא מַיָּא וְכָבָה לְנוּרָא.
D'söraf l'chutröh. D'hiköh l'chalbö.  דְּשָׂרַף לְחוּטְרָא. דְּהִכָּה לְכַלְבָּא.
D'nöshach l'shunrö. D'öch'löh  דְּנָשַׁךְ לְשׁוּנְרָא. דְּאָכְלָה
l'gad-yö. D'zabin aböh bis'ray zuzay.  לְגַדְיָא. דְּזַבִּין אַבָּא בִּתְרֵי זוּזֵי.
Chad gad-yö. Chad gad-yö.  חַד גַּדְיָא. חַד גַּדְיָא :

V'ösö sorö v'shösö l'ma-yöh.  וְאָתָא תוֹרָא וְשָׁתָה לְמַיָּא.
D'chövö l'nuröh. D'söraf  דְּכָבָה לְנוּרָא. דְּשָׂרַף
l'chutröh. D'hiköh l'chalbö.  לְחוּטְרָא. דְּהִכָּה לְכַלְבָּא.
D'nöshach l'shunrö. D'öch'löh  דְּנָשַׁךְ לְשׁוּנְרָא. דְּאָכְלָה
l'gad-yö. D'zabin aböh bis'ray zuzay.  לְגַדְיָא. דְּזַבִּין אַבָּא בִּתְרֵי זוּזֵי.
Chad gad-yö. Chad gad-yö.  חַד גַּדְיָא. חַד גַּדְיָא :

V'ösö ha-shochayt v'shöchat l'soröh.  וְאָתָא הַשּׁוֹחֵט וְשָׁחַט לְתוֹרָא.
D'shösö l'ma-yö. D'chövö l'nuröh.  דְּשָׁתָה לְמַיָּא. דְּכָבָה לְנוּרָא.
D'söraf l'chutröh. D'hiköh l'chalbö.  דְּשָׂרַף לְחוּטְרָא. דְּהִכָּה לְכַלְבָּא.
D'nöshach l'shunrö. D'öch'löh  דְּנָשַׁךְ לְשׁוּנְרָא. דְּאָכְלָה

l'gad-yö. D'zabin aböh bis'ray zuzay.
Chad gad-yö. Chad gad-yö.

לְגַדְיָא. דְּזַבִּין אַבָּא בִּתְרֵי זוּזֵי.
חַד גַּדְיָא. חַד גַּדְיָא :

V'ösö mal-ach ha-mö-ves v'shöchat
l'shochayt. D'shöchat l'soröh.
D'shösö l'ma-yö. D'chövö l'nuröh.
D'söraf l'chutröh. D'hiköh l'chalbö.
D'nöshach l'shunrö. D'öch'löh
l'gad-yö. D'zabin aböh bis'ray zuzay.
Chad gad-yö. Chad gad-yö.

וְאָתָא מַלְאַךְ הַמָּוֶת וְשָׁחַט
לְשׁוֹחֵט. דְּשָׁחַט לְתוֹרָא.
דְּשָׁתָה לְמַיָּא. דְּכָבָה לְנוּרָא.
דְּשָׂרַף לְחוּטְרָא. דְּהִכָּה לְכַלְבָּא.
דְּנָשַׁךְ לְשׁוּנְרָא. דְּאָכְלָה
לְגַדְיָא. דְּזַבִּין אַבָּא בִּתְרֵי זוּזֵי.
חַד גַּדְיָא. חַד גַּדְיָא :

V'ösö ha-ködosh böruch hu v'shöchat
l'mal-ach ha-mö-ves. D'shöchat
l'shochayt. D'shöchat l'soröh.
D'shösö l'ma-yö. D'chövö l'nuröh.
D'söraf l'chutröh. D'hiköh l'chalbö.
D'nöshach l'shunrö. D'öch'löh
l'gad-yö. D'zabin aböh bis'ray zuzay.
Chad gad-yö. Chad gad-yö.

וְאָתָא הַקָּדוֹשׁ בָּרוּךְ הוּא וְשָׁחַט
לְמַלְאַךְ הַמָּוֶת. דְּשָׁחַט
לְשׁוֹחֵט. דְּשָׁחַט לְתוֹרָא.
דְּשָׁתָה לְמַיָּא. דְּכָבָה לְנוּרָא.
דְּשָׂרַף לְחוּטְרָא. דְּהִכָּה לְכַלְבָּא.
דְּנָשַׁךְ לְשׁוּנְרָא. דְּאָכְלָה
לְגַדְיָא. דְּזַבִּין אַבָּא בִּתְרֵי זוּזֵי.
חַד גַּדְיָא. חַד גַּדְיָא :

*An only kid! That father bought for two zuzim. Then along came a cat and ate the kid. Then along came a dog and bit the cat. Then along came a stick and beat the dog. Then along came a fire and burned the stick. Then along came the water and put out the fire. Then along came an ox and drank the water. Then along came a shochet and slaughtered the ox. Then came the angel of death and felled the shochet. Then came the Holy One Blessed One, and felled the angel of death.*

143

**13.** Achas Shö-alti may-ays hashem, Osöh avakaysh, shivti b'vays hashem, köl y'may cha-yai, la-chazos b'no-am hashem, ul'vakayr b'haychölo.

אַחַת שָׁאַלְתִּי מֵאֵת ה' אוֹתָהּ אֲבַקֵּשׁ, שִׁבְתִּי בְּבֵית ה' כָּל יְמֵי חַיַּי, לַחֲזוֹת בְּנֹעַם ה' וּלְבַקֵּר בְּהֵיכָלוֹ.

*One thing I have asked of the Lord, this I seek, that I may dwell in the House of the Lord all the days of my life, to behold the pleasantness of the Lord, and to visit in His Sanctuary.*

**14.** Adon olöm asher mölach, b'terem köl y'tzur nivrö. L'ays na-asöh v'chef-tzo kol, azai melech sh'mo nikrö. V'acharay kich'los ha-kol, l'vado yimloch noröh. V'hu hö-yöh, v'hu ho-veh, v'hu yih-yeh, b'sif-öröh. V'hu echöd v'ayn shayni, l'hamshil lo l'hachbiröh. B'li rayshis b'li sachlis, v'lo hö-oz v'hamisröh. V'hu kayli v'chai go-ali, v'tzur chevli b'ays tzöröh. V'hu nisi umönos li, m'nös li m'nos kosi b'yom ekrö. B'yödo afkid ruchi, b'ays ishan v'ö-iröh. V'im ruchi g'vi-yösi, hashem li v'lo irö.

אֲדוֹן עוֹלָם אֲשֶׁר מָלַךְ, בְּטֶרֶם כָּל יְצוּר נִבְרָא. לְעֵת נַעֲשָׂה בְחֶפְצוֹ כֹּל, אֲזַי מֶלֶךְ שְׁמוֹ נִקְרָא. וְאַחֲרֵי כִּכְלוֹת הַכֹּל, לְבַדּוֹ יִמְלוֹךְ נוֹרָא. וְהוּא הָיָה, וְהוּא הֹוֶה, וְהוּא יִהְיֶה, בְּתִפְאָרָה. וְהוּא אֶחָד וְאֵין שֵׁנִי, לְהַמְשִׁיל לוֹ לְהַחְבִּירָה. בְּלִי רֵאשִׁית בְּלִי תַכְלִית, וְלוֹ הָעֹז וְהַמִּשְׂרָה. וְהוּא קֵלִי וְחַי גֹּאֲלִי, וְצוּר חֶבְלִי בְּעֵת צָרָה. וְהוּא נִסִּי וּמָנוּס לִי, מְנָת כּוֹסִי בְּיוֹם אֶקְרָא. בְּיָדוֹ אַפְקִיד רוּחִי, בְּעֵת אִישָׁן וְאָעִירָה. וְעִם רוּחִי גְּוִיָּתִי, ה' לִי וְלֹא אִירָא.

*Lord of the universe, Who reigned before anything was created — at the time when by His will all things were made, then was His Name proclaimed King. And after all things shall cease to be, the Awesome One will reign alone. He was, He is, and*

*He shall be in glory. He is one, and there is no other to compare to Him, to consort with Him. Without beginning, without end, power and dominion belong to Him. He is my God and my ever-living Redeemer, the strength of my lot in time of distress. He is my banner and my refuge, my portion on the day I call. Into His hand I entrust my spirit, when I sleep and when I awake. And with my soul, my body too, the Lord is with me, I shall not fear.*

**15.** Al tirö mipachad pis-om,    אַל תִּירָא מִפַּחַד פִּתְאֹם,
u-misho-as r'shö-im ki sövo.    וּמִשֹּׁאַת רְשָׁעִים כִּי תָבֹא.
U-tzu aytzöh v'suför, dab'ru dövör    עֻצוּ עֵצָה וְתֻפָר, דַּבְּרוּ דָבָר
v'lo yökum, ki imönu kayl.    וְלֹא יָקוּם, כִּי עִמָּנוּ קֵל.

*Do not fear sudden terror, nor the destruction of the wicked when it comes. Contrive a scheme, but it will be foiled; conspire a plot, but it will not materialize, for God is with us.*

**16.** Al ha-sela höch    עַל הַסֶּלַע הָךְ
va-yay-tz'-u mö-yim.    וַיֵּצְאוּ מָיִם.

*He struck the rock and there streamed forth water.*

**17.** Am yisrö-ayl chai.    עַם יִשְׂרָאֵל חַי.
Od övinu chai.    עוֹד אָבִינוּ חַי.

*The people of Israel live. Our Father still lives.*

145

18. Ani ma-amin be-emunöh
sh'laymöh b'vi-as ha-möshi-ach. V'af al
pi she-yismah-may-ah im köl zeh
achakeh lo b'chöl yom she-yövo.

אֲנִי מַאֲמִין בֶּאֱמוּנָה שְׁלֵמָה
בְּבִיאַת הַמָּשִׁיחַ. וְאַף עַל
פִּי שֶׁיִּתְמַהְמֵהַּ עִם כָּל זֶה
אֲחַכֶּה לּוֹ בְּכָל יוֹם שֶׁיָּבֹא.

*I believe with perfect faith in the coming of the Messiah; and although he may tarry, I will wait daily for his coming.*

19. Asher börö söson v'simchöh,
chösön v'chalöh, gilöh rinöh di-tzö
v'chedvöh, ahavöh v'achavöh
sholom v'rayus.

אֲשֶׁר בָּרָא שָׂשׂוֹן וְשִׂמְחָה
חָתָן וְכַלָּה, גִּילָה רִנָּה דִּיצָה
וְחֶדְוָה, אַהֲבָה וְאַחֲוָה
שָׁלוֹם וְרֵעוּת.

*[Blessed are You] Who created joy and happiness, groom and bride, gladness, jubilation, cheer and delight, love, friendship, harmony and fellowship.*

20. Ashraynu mah tov chelkaynu,
u-mah nö-im gorölaynu,
u-mah yöföh y'rushö-saynu.

אַשְׁרֵינוּ מַה טּוֹב חֶלְקֵנוּ,
וּמַה נָּעִים גּוֹרָלֵנוּ,
וּמַה יָּפָה יְרֻשָּׁתֵנוּ.

*Fortunate are we! How good is our portion, how pleasant our lot and how beautiful our heritage!*

21. Atöh v'chartönu miköl hö-amim,
öhavtö osönu v'rö-tzisö bönu,
v'romam-tönu miköl ha-l'shonos,
v'kidash-tönu b'mitzvo-sechö,

אַתָּה בְחַרְתָּנוּ מִכָּל הָעַמִּים,
אָהַבְתָּ אוֹתָנוּ וְרָצִיתָ בָּנוּ,
וְרוֹמַמְתָּנוּ מִכָּל הַלְּשׁוֹנוֹת,
וְקִדַּשְׁתָּנוּ בְּמִצְוֹתֶיךָ,

v'kayrav-tönu malkaynu וְקֵרַבְתָּנוּ מַלְכֵּנוּ
la-avodö-sechö, v'shim'chö לַעֲבֹדָתֶךָ, וְשִׁמְךָ
hagödol v'haködosh ölaynu körösö. הַגָּדוֹל וְהַקָּדוֹשׁ עָלֵינוּ קָרָאתָ.

*You have chosen us from among all the nations; You have loved us and found favor with us. You have raised us above all tongues and made us holy through Your commandments. You, our King, have drawn us near to Your service and proclaimed Your great and holy Name upon us.*

22. Ayleh chö-m'döh libi, אֵלֶּה חָמְדָה לִבִּי,
v'chusöh nö v'al tis-alaim. וְחוּסָה נָא וְאַל תִּתְעַלֵּם.

*These are the desires of my heart. Have mercy and turn not away from us.*

23. Dövid melech yisrö-ayl דָּוִד מֶלֶךְ יִשְׂרָאֵל
chai v'ka-yöm. חַי וְקַיָּם.

*David, King of Israel, is living and enduring.*

24. Ha-l'lu es hashem, köl go-yim, הַלְלוּ אֶת ה', כָּל גּוֹיִם,
shab'chuhu köl hö-umim. Ki gövar שַׁבְּחוּהוּ כָּל הָאֻמִּים. כִּי גָבַר
ölaynu chasdo, ve-emes hashem עָלֵינוּ חַסְדּוֹ, וֶאֱמֶת ה'
l'olöm, ha-l'luköh. לְעוֹלָם, הַלְלוּיָהּ.

*Praise the Lord, all you nations; extol Him, all you peoples. For His kindness was mighty over us, and the truth of the Lord is everlasting. Praise the Lord.*

25. Hinay mah tov umah nö-im הִנֵּה מַה טּוֹב וּמַה נָּעִים
sheves achim gam yöchad. שֶׁבֶת אַחִים גַּם יָחַד.

*How good and pleasant it is when brothers live together in harmony.*

147

**26.** Hoshi-öh es amechö, uvöraych
es nachalösechö, ur'aym
v'nas'aym ad hö-olöm.

הוֹשִׁיעָה אֶת עַמֶּךָ, וּבָרֵךְ
אֶת נַחֲלָתֶךָ, וּרְעֵם
וְנַשְּׂאֵם עַד הָעוֹלָם.

*Save Your people and bless Your possession; tend them and sustain them forever.*

**27.** Im atem m'sham'rim nayros
shel shabös, ani mar-eh löchem
nayros shel tziyon.

אִם אַתֶּם מְשַׁמְּרִים נֵרוֹת
שֶׁל שַׁבָּת, אֲנִי מַרְאֶה לָכֶם
נֵרוֹת שֶׁל צִיּוֹן.

*If you uphold the Lights of Shabbat, then I will show you the Lights of Zion.*

**28.** Ki mitziyon taytzay soröh,
ud'var hashem mi-rushölö-yim.

כִּי מִצִּיּוֹן תֵּצֵא תוֹרָה,
וּדְבַר ה' מִירוּשָׁלָיִם.

*For from Zion shall go forth the Torah, and the word of the Lord from Jerusalem.*

**29.** Köl hö-olöm kulo gesher tzar
m'od. V'hö-ikör lo l'fachayd k'löl.

כָּל הָעוֹלָם כֻּלּוֹ גֶּשֶׁר צַר
מְאֹד. וְהָעִיקָר לֹא לְפַחֵד כְּלָל.

*The whole world is a very narrow bridge, but the main thing is not to fear at all.*

**30.** L'ma-an achai v'ray-öy, adab'röh
nö shölom böch. L'ma-an bays
hashem elokaynu avak'shöh tov löch.

לְמַעַן אַחַי וְרֵעָי, אֲדַבְּרָה
נָּא שָׁלוֹם בָּךְ. לְמַעַן בֵּית
ה' אֱלֹקֵינוּ, אֲבַקְשָׁה טוֹב לָךְ.

*For the sake of my brethren and friends, I ask that there be peace within you. For the sake of the House of the Lord our God, I seek your well-being.*

31. Lo yisö goy el goy cherev
v'lo yil-m'du od milchömöh.

לֹא יִשָּׂא גוֹי אֶל גוֹי חֶרֶב
וְלֹא יִלְמְדוּ עוֹד מִלְחָמָה.

*Nation will not lift sword against nation, and they will no longer learn of war.*

32. La-y'hudim hö-y'söh o-röh
v'simchöh, v'söson vikör.
Kayn tih-yeh lönu.

לַיְהוּדִים הָיְתָה אוֹרָה
וְשִׂמְחָה, וְשָׂשֹׂן וִיקָר.
כֵּן תִּהְיֶה לָּנוּ.

*For the Jews there was light and joy, gladness and honor, so let it be with us.*

33. Mal'chus'chö mal'chus köl
olömim, umem-shal-t'chö
b'chöl dor vödor.

מַלְכוּתְךָ מַלְכוּת כָּל
עֹלָמִים, וּמֶמְשַׁלְתְּךָ
בְּכָל דּוֹר וָדֹר.

*Your kingship is a kingship over all worlds, and Your dominion is throughout all generations.*

34. Mi-mitzra-yim g'altönu,
mi-bays avödim, p'disönu.

מִמִּצְרַיִם גְּאַלְתָּנוּ,
מִבֵּית עֲבָדִים פְּדִיתָנוּ.

*You have delivered us from Egypt, redeemed us from the house of bondage.*

35. Min ha-maytzar körösi köh,
önöni va-merchav köh.

מִן הַמֵּצַר קָרָאתִי קָּהּ,
עָנָּנִי בַמֶּרְחַב קָהּ.

*From out of distress I called to God; with abounding relief, God answered me.*

36. M'kimi may-öför döl.

מְקִימִי מֵעָפָר דָּל.

*He raises the poor from the dust.*

**37.** Od yishōma b'öray y'hudöh
uv'chu-tzos y'rushölö-yim, kol söson
v'kol simchöh, kol chösön
v'kol kalöh.

עוֹד יִשָּׁמַע בְּעָרֵי יְהוּדָה
וּבְחוּצוֹת יְרוּשָׁלָיִם, קוֹל שָׂשׂוֹן
וְקוֹל שִׂמְחָה, קוֹל חָתָן
וְקוֹל כַּלָּה.

*May there still be heard in the cities of Judah and in the streets of Jerusalem the sound of joy and the sound of happiness, the sound of a groom and the sound of a bride.*

**38.** Or zöru-ah latzadik,
ul'yish'ray layv simchöh.

אוֹר זָרֻעַ לַצַּדִּיק,
וּלְיִשְׁרֵי לֵב שִׂמְחָה.

*Light is sown for the righteous, and joy for the upright in heart.*

**39.** O-seh shölom bim'romöv,
hu ya-aseh shölom ölaynu,
v'al köl yisrö-ayl, v'im'ru ömayn.

עֹשֶׂה שָׁלוֹם בִּמְרוֹמָיו,
הוּא יַעֲשֶׂה שָׁלוֹם עָלֵינוּ,
וְעַל כָּל יִשְׂרָאֵל וְאִמְרוּ אָמֵן.

*He Who makes peace in His heavens, may He make peace for us and for all Israel; and say, Amen.*

**40.** Övinu malkaynu ayn lönu
melech elö ötöh.

אָבִינוּ מַלְכֵּנוּ אֵין לָנוּ
מֶלֶךְ אֶלָּא אָתָּה.

*Our Father our King, we have no King but You.*

**41.** Övinu malkaynu chönaynu אָבִינוּ מַלְכֵּנוּ חָנֵּנוּ
va-anaynu ki ayn bönu ma-asim, וַעֲנֵנוּ כִּי אֵין בָּנוּ מַעֲשִׂים,
asay imönu tz'dököh vöchesed עֲשֵׂה עִמָּנוּ צְדָקָה וָחֶסֶד
v'hoshi-aynu. וְהוֹשִׁיעֵנוּ.

*Our Father, our King, be gracious to us and answer us, for we have no meritorious deeds; for the sake of Your great Name, deal charitably and kindly with us and deliver us.*

**42.** She-yibö-neh bays ha-mikdösh שֶׁיִּבָּנֶה בֵּית הַמִּקְדָּשׁ
bim'hayröh v'yömaynu, v'sayn בִּמְהֵרָה בְיָמֵינוּ, וְתֵן
chelkaynu b'sorösechö. חֶלְקֵנוּ בְּתוֹרָתֶךָ.

*[May it be Your will] that the Beis Hamikdosh (Holy Temple) be speedily rebuilt in our days, and grant us our portion in Your Torah.*

**43.** Sh'ma yisrö-ayl, hashem שְׁמַע יִשְׂרָאֵל, ה'
elokaynu, hashem echöd. אֱלֹקֵינוּ, ה' אֶחָד.

*Hear, O Israel, the Lord is our God, the Lord is One.*

**44.** Simön tov uma-zöl tov y'hay סִמָּן טוֹב וּמַזָּל טוֹב יְהֵא
lö-nu ul'chöl yisrö-ayl ömayn. לָנוּ וּלְכָל יִשְׂרָאֵל אָמֵן.

*May there be a good omen and good mazal for us and for all Israel. Amen.*

**45.** ufö-ratztö yömöh vökayd-möh וּפָרַצְתָּ יָמָּה וָקֵדְמָה
v'tzöfonöh vö-negböh. וְצָפֹנָה וָנֶגְבָּה.

*And you shall spread forth to the west, and to the east, and to the north, and to the south.*

**46.** Uv'nay y'rushöla-yim ir ha-kodesh bim'hayröh v'yömaynu.

וּבְנֵה יְרוּשָׁלַיִם עִיר הַקֹּדֶשׁ בִּמְהֵרָה בְיָמֵינוּ.

*And rebuild Jerusalem the holy city speedily in our days.*

**47.** V'hö-ayr aynay-nu b'sorösechö v'dabayk li-baynu b'mitzvo-sechö, v'yachyd l'vövaynu l'ahavöh ul'yir-öh es sh'mechö. V'lo nayvosh, v'lo nikölaym, v'lo niköshayl l'olöm vö-ed. Ki v'shaym köd-sh'chö ha-gödol v'ha-noröh bötöch-nu, nögilö v'nism'chö bishu-ösechö.

וְהָאֵר עֵינֵינוּ בְּתוֹרָתֶךָ וְדַבֵּק לִבֵּנוּ בְּמִצְוֹתֶיךָ, וְיַחֵד לְבָבֵנוּ לְאַהֲבָה וּלְיִרְאָה אֶת שְׁמֶךָ. וְלֹא נֵבוֹשׁ, וְלֹא נִכָּלֵם, וְלֹא נִכָּשֵׁל, לְעוֹלָם וָעֶד. כִּי בְשֵׁם קָדְשְׁךָ הַגָּדוֹל וְהַנּוֹרָא בָּטָחְנוּ, נָגִילָה וְנִשְׂמְחָה בִּישׁוּעָתֶךָ.

*Enlighten our eyes in Your Torah, cause our hearts to cleave to Your commandments, and unite our hearts to love and fear Your Name, and may we never be put to shame, disgrace or stumbling. Because we trust in Your holy, great and awesome Name, may we rejoice and exult in Your salvation.*

**48.** V'sömachtö b'chagechö v'hö-yisö ach sömay-ach.

וְשָׂמַחְתָּ בְּחַגֶּךָ וְהָיִיתָ אַךְ שָׂמֵחַ.

*Rejoice in your Festival, and you shall be altogether joyful.*

**49.** Yibö-neh ha-mikdösh, ir tziyon t'malay, v'shöm nöshir shir chödösh uvir'nönöh na-aleh.

יִבָּנֶה הַמִּקְדָּשׁ, עִיר צִיּוֹן תְּמַלֵּא, וְשָׁם נָשִׁיר שִׁיר חָדָשׁ וּבִרְנָנָה נַעֲלֶה.

*The Temple will be rebuilt, the city of Zion will be replenished, and there we shall sing a new song, and with praise we will go up.*

**50.** Yis-m'chu ha-shoma-yim v'sögayl hö-öretz, yir-am ha-yöm um'lo-o.   יִשְׂמְחוּ הַשָּׁמַיִם וְתָגֵל הָאָרֶץ, יִרְעַם הַיָּם וּמְלֹאוֹ.

*The heavens will rejoice, the earth will exult; the sea and its fullness will roar.*

**51.** Yisrö-ayl b'tach ba-shem, ezröm umöginöm hu.   יִשְׂרָאֵל בְּטַח בַּה', עֶזְרָם וּמָגִנָּם הוּא.

*Israel trusts in the Lord; He is their help and protector.*

**52.** Y'min hashem romaymöh, y'min hashem osöh chö-yil.   יְמִין ה' רוֹמֵמָה, יְמִין ה' עֹשָׂה חָיִל.

*The right hand of the Lord is exalted; the right hand of the Lord performs deeds of valor.*

**53.** Y'vörech'chö hashem mitziyon, ur'ay b'tuv y'rushölö-yim kol y'may cha-yechö. Ur'ay vönim l'vönechö, shölom al yisrö-ayl.   יְבָרֶכְךָ ה' מִצִּיּוֹן, וּרְאֵה בְּטוּב יְרוּשָׁלָיִם כֹּל יְמֵי חַיֶּיךָ. וּרְאֵה בָנִים לְבָנֶיךָ, שָׁלוֹם עַל יִשְׂרָאֵל.

*May the Lord bless you from Zion and may you see the prosperity of Jerusalem all the days of your life. May you live to see your children's children. May Israel have peace.*

# Passover Glossary

**Afikoman**: (lit, "dessert,") from the Aramaic *fiku man*, "bring out the food" the portion of matzah eaten at the close of the seder meal in commemoration of the Passover offering.

**Baytzah**: egg.

**Bedikat chometz**: the search for leaven conducted on the night before Passover eve.

**Beirach**: (lit. "bless") the thirteenth activity of the seder — recitation of Grace After Meals.

**Bet HaMikdash**: Holy Temple in Jerusalem.

**Birkat Hamazon**: Grace After Meals.

**Chagigah**: the festival offering.

**Chometz**: leavened foods; fermented or leavened wheat, rye, oats, spelt and barley, prohibited on Passover.

**The Burning of:** All chometz in one's possession must be destroyed before Passover (unless it was sold to a non-Jew, see "The Sale of Chometz").

**The Nullification of:** Since chometz may not be held in one's possession during Passover, one may rid oneself of the chometz by declaring all types of chometz in one's possession to be abandoned property. This is done before Passover.

**That Wasn't Sold or Destroyed:** Any chometz held over Passover under Jewish ownership may not be used or sold after Passover. It is to be discarded.

**The Sale of:** Chometz that has been transferred to a non-Jew need not be destroyed. This transfer is traditionally carried out by engaging the Rabbi to act as an agent to sell the chometz to a non-Jew. Chometz that has been sold must be put in a completely sealed-off place, inaccessible during Passover.

**The Search for:** On the night before Passover, a search for chometz is to be conducted in the home wherever chometz may have been brought during the year. Chometz found during the search is set aside for burning the next day.

**Charoset**: a paste made of apples, pears, nuts and wine, in which the maror is dipped.

**Chazeret**: (lit. "lettuce") vegetable used for moror (bitter herbs)

**Chol HaMoed**: (lit. "mundane [days] of the festival") the intermediate days of the Festivals of Passover and Succot.

**Da-yaynu**: "It is enough for us" – the refrain from a song in the Haggadah.

**Erev**: (lit. "eve of") day preceding Shabbat or Festivals.

**Haggadah**: (lit. "narration") the text that is recited at the seder.

**Halachah**: (lit. "the pathway") the entire body of Jewish law; a specific law.

**Hallel**: (lit. "praise") the 14th activity of the seder – reciting the Hallel, Psalms of praise and thanksgiving to God.

**Hashem**: (lit. "The Name") God.

**Havdalah**: (lit. separation) the blessings recited at the conclusion of Shabbat and Festivals, separating the holy day from the other days of the week.

**Kadesh**: (lit. "sanctify") the first activity of the seder – to recite the Kiddush.

**Karpas**: (lit. "greens") the vegetable, dipped in saltwater, eaten at the beginning of the seder.

**Ke'ara**: (lit. "plate") the tray, plate or cloth on which are placed the three matzot and six items for use during the seder.

**Kezayit**: (lit. "like an olive") a Halachic measurement, approx. 1 oz.

**Kiddush**: (lit. "sanctification") the sanctification of Shabbat and Festivals with a blessing recited over a cup of wine.

**Kitniot**: Leguminous vegetables such as beans, peas, corn and rice. The consumption of these foods is restricted by European Rabbinic tradition, though these foods are not chometz. Yeminite, Sephardic and Oriental Jews are not bound to this custom.

**Korech**: (lit. "wrap", "make a sandwich") the tenth activity of the seder – to eat matzah and maror combined in a sandwich.

**Maggid**: (lit. "telling") the fifth activity of the seder – the telling of the story of the Exodus.

**Maror**: bitter herbs.

**Matzah**: (pl. **matzot**) unleavened bread.

**Mayim acharonim**: (lit. "last water") the practice, mandated by Torah law, to wash the tips of one's fingers at the conclusion of a meal.

**Midrash**: the non-literal interpretation and homiletic teachings of the Sages, on Scripture.

**Mishnah**: the codification of the Oral Law that forms the crux of the Talmud, or a specific paragraph of that work.

**Mitzrayim**: Egypt.

**Mitzvah**: (pl. **Mitzvot**) "commandment"; the precepts of the Torah; also "good deed".

**Moshiach**: (lit. "the annointed") the Messiah.

**Motzi**: (lit. "take out" or "bring forth") the blessing, thanking God "Who brings forth bread from the earth," recited before eating bread or matzah.

**Nissan**: the Hebrew month in which Passover falls; mandated by the Torah to occur in the (beginning of) spring.

**Rachtzah**: (lit. "washing") the sixth activity of the seder — washing before eating the matzah.

**Seder**: (lit. "order") the gathering and meal which takes place on the first two nights of Passover and follows a specific order.

**Shabbat**: (lit: "rest", "cessation [of work]") the Sabbath; the divinely-ordained day of rest on the seventh day of the week.

**Shechinah**: (lit. "indwelling", "immanence") the Divine Presence; that aspect of the Divine which resides within, or is in any way connected with, the created reality.

**Shmurah matzah**: (lit. "watched" or "guarded" matzah) Matzah which has been made from grain which was guarded from the time of either reaping or grinding to ensure that it never came into contact with water or other liquids, to prevent it from rising.

**Shulchan Orech**: (lit: "set table") the eleventh activity of the seder — eating the festive meal.

**Siddur:** (lit. "ordering", "arrangement") the prayer book.

**Torah:** (lit. "law", "instruction") the Divine wisdom and will communicated to Moses and handed down through the generations; includes both the "Written Torah" (the Tanach or "Bible") and the "Oral Torah" (the interpretation and exposition of the Written Torah, as recorded in the Talmud, the Torah commentaries, the Halachic works, the Kabbalah, etc.).

**Tzafun:** (lit. "hidden") the twelfth activity of the seder — to eat the *Afikoman* which has been hidden away since the beginning of the seder.

**Tzedakah:** (lit. justice, righteousness) charity.

**Urchatz:** (lit: "and wash") the second activity of the seder — washing one's hands before eating the karpas.

**Yachatz:** (lit: "divide") the fourth activity of the seder — breaking the middle matzah in two.

**Yom Tov:** (lit. "a good day") a festival on the Jewish calendar.

**Zeroah:** (lit: "shank bone") the first item on the seder plate, commemorating the Passover offering; can be any bone with a bit of kosher meat — although a chicken neck is commonly used.

*Special credit to www.Passover.net for portions of this glossary*

# לזכות

הרב יוסף בן חי׳ מלכה
מרת חנה פריווא בת אלטער יהושע הכהן
הרב שניאור זלמן בן חנה פריווא
מרת דבורה גבריאלה בת רייזא פייגא
מנחם מענדל בן מרים שרה
מניא שיינא בת מרים שרה
חנה פריווא בת דבורה גבריאלה

# More from our Companion Series

**The Shabbat Table Companion: Transliterated Kiddush, Bencher, and Songs**
This guide features easy-to-read English transliterations, concise explanations, plus over 140 popular Shabbat and Yom Tov table songs to help create a true Shabbat atmosphere in your home. *Softcover; 6.5x5.5; 160 pages; JLG-01; ISBN 1-891293-11-7. (Audio available)*

**The Shabbat Synagogue Companion: Explains Prayers for Shabbat Eve and Shabbat Day**
A complete guide to both Friday evening and Shabbat morning prayer services, the Companion maps every prayer and explains its origin and meaning. It includes English transliterations of many key prayers and instructions for performing common synagogue honors such as opening the Ark and being called to the Torah. *Softcover; 6.5x5.5; 160 pages; JLG-02; ISBN 1-891293-12-5.*

**The Kabbalat Shabbat Synagogue Companion: Transliterations and Explanations**
Presenting the complete Friday evening service, along with easy-to-read English transliterations, clear instructions, and a concise overview of Shabbat and prayer. This plain language guide will enable you to pray, sing, and comprehend the services at a higher level. *Softcover; 6.5x5.5; 160 pages; JLG-04; ISBN 1-891293-14-1. (Audio available)*

**The Complete Junior Congregation Synagogue Companion: For Children in the Synagogue**
Designed for beginners of all ages, this companion brings the Shabbat synagogue experience to life. It features the basic Shabbat prayers in clear Hebrew type, alongside easy-to-read English transliterations, and easy to understand English translations and explanations so everyone will be able to join in and enjoy the prayer services like never before. *Softcover; 6.5x5.5; 160 pages; JLG-08; ISBN 1-891293-19-2.*

**The High Holiday Synagogue Companion: Transliterations and Explanations**
Your personal guide to and through the Rosh Hashanah and Yom Kippur prayerbook. It explains what prayers are found on each page, their origin, meaning, and the proper action required at each point, and includes key prayers as well as many inspirational readings and stories. *Softcover; JLG-03; ISBN 1-891293-10-9.*

**The Complete Jewish Wedding Companion: Guide to a Traditional Jewish Wedding**
The ultimate guide to understanding and enjoying a traditional Jewish wedding experience. Contains clear instructions, explanations, and directions, plus all relevant prayers, liturgy, and blessings. *Softcover; 6.5x5.5; 128 pages; JLG-07; ISBN 1-891293-18-4*